ALSO BY JAMES SCHUYLER

POEMS

May 24th, or So (1966)

Freely Espousing (1969)

The Crystal Lithium (1972)

Hymn to Life (1974)

The Morning of the Poem (1980)

A Few Days (1985)

Selected Poems (1988; 2007)

Collected Poems (1993)

NOVELS

Alfred and Guinevere (1958)

A Nest of Ninnies (with John Ashbery, 1976)

What's for Dinner? (1978)

MISCELLANEOUS

The Home Book (edited by Trevor Winkfield, 1977)

The Diary of James Schuyler (edited by Nathan Kernan, 1996)

Selected Art Writings (edited by Simon Pettet, 1998)

Just the Thing: Selected Letters of James Schuyler (edited by William
     Corbett, 2004)

OTHER FLOWERS

Other Flowers

UNCOLLECTED POEMS

James Schuyler

EDITED BY JAMES MEETZE AND SIMON PETTET

Farrar, Straus and Giroux
New York

Farrar, Straus and Giroux
18 West 18th Street, New York 10011

Some of these poems first appeared in the following publications: *The American Poetry Review* ("Far Off," "Letter Poem to Kenneth Koch," "Miss Weevy: Will She Make Out All Right?," "Poem (I feel I know you very well)," and "There Is a Certain Something"), *The Georgia Review* ("Atlantic Snore" and "Via della Vite"), *Granta* ("Coming Night" and "Mother's Land"), *Harper's Magazine* ("Africa! Africa!"), *Maggy* ("Catalog," "The Gate to the Lake," "Gifts," and "Poem (Between glacier and glacier)"), *The Nation* ("The Smallest"), *The New Yorker* ("Love's Photograph (*or* Father and Son)"), *Open City* ("Birdland (*or* Caligula-Caligulee, or Come into the Garden Maud, the Grass Needs Mowing)," "It's Nice Inside When It Snows," "Small Talk," and "To Jorge in Sickness"), *The Paris Review* ("'Dedicated to G. Verdi. Because It's His Birthday.'" "Distraction: An Ode," "Invocation," "Like (Sonnet fragment)," "Starlings," and "Where Was I?"), *Poetry* ("Address," "Destitute Peru," "Foreign Parts," "Last Night," "Poem (The day gets slowly started)," "Scarlatti," and "Tears, Oily Tears . . ."), and *A Public Space* ("The Home" and "We See Us as We Truly Behave").

Library of Congress Cataloging-in-Publication Data
Schuyler, James.
    Other flowers : uncollected poems / James Schuyler ; edited by James Meetze,
  Simon Pettet.— 1st ed.
      p.   cm.
    Includes index.
    ISBN 978-0-374-53209-3 (hardcover)
    I. Meetze, James, 1977–   II. Pettet, Simon.   III. Title.

PS3569.C56 O75 2010
811'.54—dc22

                                                                            2009031891

www.fsgbooks.com

10   9   8   7   6   5   4   3   2   1

for Darragh Park

CONTENTS

"What other flowers are there?" James Schuyler asks in his poem "Catalog" (included here on p. 148), as if to remind us that what is initially shown isn't, necessarily, the complete picture. So it is not a surprise to find that the poems that constituted his published oeuvre (the *Collected Poems*—Farrar, Straus and Giroux, 1993), are not, and were not, the only ones. In fact, a veritable English country garden's worth of poetry and fragments had been idly waiting among papers and ephemera in the Mandeville Special Collections Library at the University of California, San Diego. It was among these papers that, in February 2005, the poems comprising this volume were found. I had just moved to San Diego from San Francisco, in part to study the James Schuyler Papers, however unsure of what it was I might find there. In the archive, I came upon boxes marked "Miscellaneous Collected Poems," each containing folders noted "Unpublished." Over the following four months, as I read through the myriad typescripts—many of which appeared in multiple drafts—and handwritten notebooks, I began to truly understand the melancholy of unfound treasures, and the wealth inherent in their subsequent unveiling.

These poems so astonished me with their quality, their clarity, their classic "Schuylerian detail"—there is none quite like it—that it seemed there was a poignancy in their having been hidden so long. Though none were included in any of his published collections, they are rich and representative of his entire career, evoked by his various muses: friends, lovers, nature, weather, music, and art. Schuyler acknowledges the nature of his palette, noting, "It is infinite and therefore the smallest thing" ("The Smallest," p. 170). It is this acknowledgment that makes the organic processes of his writing so consistently human and so startlingly reverberant.

Born on November 9, 1923, in Chicago, Illinois, James Marcus Schuyler was raised in the suburb of Downers Grove, which he remembers vividly in the poem "Snapshot" (p. 4): "There were wood-slat

sidewalks / and there are photographs / of me in white dresses."
When he was six, his family moved to Washington, D.C., where
his father took a job at *The Washington Star*. His parents, Marcus
Schuyler and Margaret Connor Schuyler, divorced shortly thereafter.
In 1931, she married Frederic Ridenour, with whom she and the
young James later moved to Buffalo, New York, settling in the suburb
of East Aurora, where Schuyler spent his teenage years (see "East Au-
rora," his extraordinary poem of youthful memory, beginning on
p. 13). It was here that he discovered a love of reading and the desire
to write, though his stepfather was singularly unsupportive. During
this time, he came to acknowledge and accept his homosexuality
(which would later become a defining fact of his character and in-
deed an integral, even joyful, part of his work). He approached the
erotic with the same exuberant regard as he would a landscape (or
anything else, for that matter): "the fullness of his lower lip, like
the excess that shaped the pear, sulky / and determined, boyish and
sweet" ("Having My Say-so," p. 47).

Schuyler enrolled at Bethany College in West Virginia in 1941,
but stayed for only two years and then joined the Navy. In the poem
"Great Spruce Head Key West" (p. 100), he remembers his time at
the Fleet Sonar School in Key West (which Frank O'Hara attended a
year later), "Dawn smites, storms, and the sea, / molten at dusk,"
"the condemned men laughed, sailed." Schuyler served on the USS
Glennon, doing convoy duty in the North Atlantic. However, this,
and any thoughts of a naval career, came to an abrupt end when he
got recklessly drunk while on shore leave and went AWOL in New
York City. He was discharged from the Navy in 1944. From then on,
he devoted himself full-time to art, as a writer.

In 1947, with his firebrand lover Bill Aalto, Schuyler traveled
to Italy. The following year, at the invitation of his friend Chester
Kallman, lover and companion to the poet W. H. Auden, Schuyler
and Aalto traveled to Ischia, where they stayed at Auden's island
home. Here, as a favor to Auden, Schuyler would type the poems that
would become the manuscript of Auden's book *Nones* (1951). Schuy-
ler eulogizes the three, and recollects his own past, in "Poem (We all lay

on the island beach together)" (p. 94)—"now they are gone. . . . // Leukemia took Bill. Wystan and Chester / passed on, as they say, in sleep. I bid / them adieu."

Schuyler returned to New York in the summer of 1949. Two years later, he met fellow poets and lifelong friends Frank O'Hara and John Ashbery at the Tibor de Nagy Gallery opening for Larry Rivers's first exhibition of paintings—a singular moment, in retrospect, in the crucial constellation that became the fabled "New York School." It was O'Hara's poem "The Three-Penny Opera"—a gossipy meditation on Brecht ("I think a lot about / the Peachums: Polly / and all the rest . . .")—that, Schuyler later confessed, first inspired him to begin seriously attempting poetry (prior to that, he had been principally a short-story writer). There are countless instances of O'Hara's influence on the early work here. The way images and speech, for example, enter extempore: "It clears away: the rain / is only rain that didn't fall. / I got my hair cut. / The night, well it's another / windy mess" (from "Distraction: An Ode," p. 24). It was his relationship to painting and painters, however—in particular, Fairfield Porter—that influenced his poetry most significantly. As Porter remarked of his own painting, "I think that what would satisfy me is to . . . make everything more beautiful." The same could also be said of Schuyler's poetry. His gestural line contains a transparent gravity that never tries to add weight to what he sees, but tethers it to earth. In "A Blue Shadow Painting" (p. 76), he writes of the "dark there-ness / of the tree, malleable steel-gray blueness of the ground; and sky; / set against, no, with, living with, existing alongside of and part of / . . . swift indecipherables." He is not only describing a painting but doing something more profound, expressing the relationship of art to the world, and how, for him, art and life are inseparable.

Most everyone and every place Schuyler was in regular contact with—because he faithfully records what he sees—makes an appearance in one poem or another, doing what they happen to do, saying what they happen to say, being as they were, for him, literally "on display." All of this appears in the poetry as a collage of snapshots and dialogue, always with a certain warmth, as if to map his existence, and leaving breadcrumbs behind for someone like me, who, though I never knew the "Jimmy" of these poems, feel as if I did. Schuyler's quiet intimacy is welcoming. A James Schuyler poem invites us to open our eyes to the intricate simplicities and exactitudes of each day, to notice how "hollyhocks sway in the wind like the masts of little sailboats" or "the sky / has been rubbed soft while the river is rough as ground glass" (p. 17).

Schuyler is a master of the paradoxical, in the sense that he can appear, at times, almost indifferent while he addresses what is most dear to him. In "Poem (Help me)" (p. 124), he writes, "the profoundest order is revealed / in what is most casual." He speaks of the way in which the untimely death of Frank O'Hara struck him (and indeed struck all of O'Hara's friends) as an intolerable blow, "when I think / of Frank and I do / a lot, my head / wants to burst / with unshed tears" (p. 126). Such moments of unflinching honesty—always at the very heart of his poems—coexist easily with the lines just prior, which address his friends, the poet Ron Padgett, and his wife, Pat, regarding their young son, Wayne: "Dear Pat'n'Ron . . . // Tell Wayne not to grow up so fast. Some of us huff / and puff a lot running to keep up" (p. 125). Such great tonal leaps are characteristic of Schuyler's integral commingling of wit and insouciance, empathy and sincerity, a hallmark of his virtuosity.

James Schuyler remains a central and inimitable figure in twentieth-century poetry. Delicate, careful, witty, and crass—often even in the same line—his poems offer astute observation capable of transporting us instantly through time and space. His is, as he puts it in the poem "Grousset's China (*or* Slogans)," "a precision of multiplicity" (p. 34). His reverence for the essence of all things, the equal care given to an island's silhouette as to a close friend's or intimate lover's form, the beauty found in things just being as they are, the celebration, shine like a beacon, as bright now as it ever was.

James Meetze
San Diego
January 2010

James Meetze's fortuitous discovery of this trove of unpublished James Schuyler poems is a major event. The absolute accomplishment of these poems (more than secondary juvenilia) is a source of incredulous delight. Who knew?—as they say—although one might have guessed. Schuyler's "first book" (not entirely such, but let's call it that), *Freely Espousing*, was published late—as late as 1969. A long, studied, rich apprenticeship and, as can be seen here, early maturity, predates it.

Other Flowers—the book's title pretty much actively asserts itself, and with an opening poem (p. 3), an invocation, a declaration to "say what I should say / in a few bright naming words." We begin, then, with a glorious signature poem (much like the more familiar "Salute"), and conclude (p. 198) with a similarly momentous, similarly timely, utterance, Schuyler's deft translation of Giacomo Leopardi— "Now rest forever / my tired heart."

And in between? Life lies in between. An inspirational miscellany, the typed manuscript was initially presented to me in simple alphabetical order. It is I who took the responsibility—the huge presumption, it should readily be confessed!—of rearranging and shaping it. Standard disclaimer: all errors or distortions or obfuscations thus created are therefore entirely my own.

The architectonics (the ordering) I follow from an earlier methodology, working much as I'd done in the likewise posthumous 1998 edition of Schuyler's *Selected Art Writings*: not entirely according to chronology, not entirely according to theme, but, I hope, at all times keenly respectful of both. Some sort of narrative is proposed so each poem follows logically the poem that precedes it. Sequential constellations propel "the story" along, but there is no insistence. Following the autobiographical early poems, there are playful early experiments (acrostics, collages, verse plays, zany epistles), parodies, and pronouncements. There is also, woven in, a sequence of love poems, dedicatory poems to friends, sonnets, sestinas, summer poems, and travel poems. Schuyler is moved, in one of his epigraphs (it's in the poem "For Reasons Not Known to Me," p. 188), to quote his friend John Ashbery: "Poems are written under many conditions." And are subsequently received, one is tempted to add, variously, at their own pace, in their own time—"go, little poem"—"*news*" that, in Ezra Pound's memorable phrase, if true, simply "*stays news.*"

The belated arrival of this gathering, then, marks another singular occasion (Schuyler's poetry delights in occasions). *Other Flowers* is a boon, a bouquet, a treat, and a treasure. What more could one ask for? His *Collected Poems* have just been pleasingly and stunningly and gorgeously expanded. Fanfare! This is indeed a cause for joy.

Simon Pettet
New York City
January 2010

OTHER FLOWERS

INVOCATION

Scatter your lines like willow leaves
        a summer storm tears at the weeping withys
sprinkle with words this sheet as the wind
        cross-ventilates and veils the yellow floor with dust
pollinate, a poem
        or at least a sneeze
the tops of the clouds are clear
        in bulk and turning edge
the bottoms are fused with sky while the Beekman Tower
        begins to burn in an evening fury
deeper than gold

        Speak
a few light words
        quick and true
as the pigment—was it pink—Felix
        Pasilis worked into the still wet ground
barely contrasted
        —who stops to count the waving willow leaves?
from here, blended strokes
        wavering for the storm is passed
summer is more than come
so come,
        say what I should say
        in a few bright naming words

SNAPSHOT

I do not remember
the house where I lived first.
I know
the small-town name,
Downers Grove, outside Chicago,
The Windy City.
There were wood-slat sidewalks
and there are photographs
of me in white dresses,
with a tin pail and shovel,
playing with a little girl.

I have on a too-big Indian suit
in one, and am laughing,
with my eyes shut,
at my mother sitting
on a little stool on the sidewalk
drying her hair
in the sunlight and laughing
at me, with a war bonnet
down around my ears.

And we had a touring car.
Then we moved
to Washington, D.C.

VIA DELLA VITE

I'm not happy.
My spirits that lifted
me so high, went off like smoke
after a shot. How can
I fear so many diverse things?
I want to think of other things.
Is it all
in how you think?
I want to think
of a washing machine
in a basement, and a woman ironing.
I can smell the wash,
I can smell the ironing.
I can see the jars of jam
on shelves, the bushels
for ashes, and the basement steps
up which I used to tote them.
I want to think
of a lawn mower, of how much I hated
cutting grass. To smell,
again,
burning leaves, or an attic
in the heat of summer.
I want to hear
the snow.

To have wished to get
so far from all that,
to get there and half-wish
I could go back
to a corner of the sloping yard

where one night
between the roof and a tree
that had funny little leaves
the moon stood bright
in a sky that still was light.

MOTHER'S LAND

Wet ashes sprout beggar's lace,
grandmothers' weed. Flowers are
weeds, they two said to tea cake
at Linden Terrace.
Lake, unleash my drowned
Minnesota, Minnesota
loons vesper the flat world,
a paper Columbian rose-base,
armadillo-shaded study lamp.
Uncle converts the croquet
wickets, his secret secret. Show
the new girl, dear, she'll learn.
Attrition: to spend a death
waiting a life. Plaited hair,
wow-boy garter girdle, tiered
here to the floor in moiré,
strewn with Bible scenes. Potiphar,
et cetera. A carnelian he swiped
in Greece, Europe, and smuggled
anally home. Great Sue, Shropshire-
sharp shears, suckled her needle
teeth in hog flesh. Painted
grapes 'round the dining room, often,
crack-back, kneeled: addressed
the Deity as three from over waves
uhm, like her. Her and He.

LOVE'S PHOTOGRAPH (*OR* FATHER AND SON)

Detected little things: a peach-pit
basket watch-chain charm, an ivory
cross wound with ivory ivy, a natural
cross. The Tatoosh Mountains, opaque
crater lakes, a knickerbockered boy
who, drowned, smiles for a seeming ever
on ice skates on ice-skate-scratched
ice, an enlarged scratched snapshot.
Taken, taken. Mad charges corrupt to
madness their sane nurses. Virginia
creeper, Loose Tooth tanned black snake-
skins, shot crows for crow wings for
a black servant's hat, lapped hot milk,
flung mud in a Bible reader's crotch:
"You shouldn't read the Bible nekkid!"
Family opals, selfishness changes hands.
Tatoosh Mountains, opaque crater lakes,
find me the fish skeleton enclosed in
a fish skeleton (fish ate fish) he had.

COMING NIGHT

It darkens, brother,
and your crutch-tip grinds
the gravel the deer stepped delicately along
one breakfast, you were a kid.
Mother says after thirty,
decades clip by
"and then you have the sum"
or spent it.

What was it like when the car
swerved on the ice,
what did you think of,
how long did you wait
in the wreck with the pain?

I see the sumacs by the turning space
turn their lank leaves,
the railway move to us
and the willows below us
and think of you turning nineteen,
of the deer, the sumac, trains, a wreck.

LIGHT NIGHT

1

A tree, enamel needles,
owl takeoffs shake,
flapping a sound and smell
of underwing, like flags,
the clothy weight of flags.
A cone of silence stuck
with diamonds, the watch
she hunts, the frayed band
broke. It was a black night.
Dawn walked on it, the sun
set its heel. She won't
find: a boundary of marsh,
the island in the wood.

2

Stoop, dove, horrid maid,
spread your chiffon on our
wood rot breeding the
Destroying Angel, white,
lathe-shapely, trout-lily
lovely. Taste, and have it.

3

In a rain-dusk dawn, the
clearing edge, the wood's
fangs, the clear crystal
twist of a salival stream,
announce you hence. Tear
free of me, mountain, old
home bone, down sheer fear

tears mossed boulders
bound me, pool, deceptive,
trout-full, laugh and
chatter of finch and pecker,
gargle my liquor skin I
catch your face on. Scar
a look and leave. A rust
plush daycoach unfathers
me. A field of crosses. Let
iron clang iron.

BLANK REGARD

Crystal flesh, starry lice,
gilded silver scows, ivory
death-mask fall feathered,
wrists' anemones, eyes' dials,
a viol slashes currant-red
damask love-seats and lapis
spittoons. Riots. Axe's drip
drip, a basket of heads. Of
embassies, of retaliant tunes,
hawkers, harpers, chronicle.
Dusty oxen scamper in hills,
greened, spiked, wheel cut.
Time, bite your tail, hoop
snake the steak-sliced neck.

EAST AURORA

Towns of a few thousand, clutched about stores and churches like points where flesh is attached to bone!

And suburbs of cities.

That there isn't more rage, slaps, curses, plates of food flung across dinner tables at familiar diners.

Pointed the hose through the kitchen window at her, so *she* threw the pot of geraniums at *him*.

Take down the old magazines from the attic and burn them, as though a photograph might tell what someone was thinking when it was looked at, umpteen years ago.

The sky changes its decoration like a housewife exchanging slip covers.

Priests play checkers. Nuns go out to the tin dairy barn to milk the cows. At the Holy Rollers, a big shout.

Another name for *portulaca* is moss rose.

A water snake in the pool lifts itself like an asparagus stalk. The pool is below a small falls that empties the pond. A sunfish tumbles and flips down the falls, from pond to pool.

He made an iris garden in a vacant lot, one of each kind of iris, just about, like a bit of Old Japan.

They went driving. The sun shone on the ice on the creeks— windows of a new house—snow streaked on the ice.

Homemade root beer explodes like giant salutes.

"Hallowe'en vandalism on upswing."

No house whose age cannot be reckoned precisely.

She takes a bath. The tub is full of her like the washing machine churning sheets on Monday. No wonder her back aches.

The dog did his business on the oriental rug again.

Right after they moved into the new house, she died. His sister came to keep house for him. He keeps his own room neatly as a sailor, which he used to be. He had her pet name not her christened name cut on the granite headstone with a chipped border as though gnawed by mice.

Linseed Oil in a bottle stoppered by a twist of rag, and oily rags in a pipe-tobacco can.

In the mist a willow is turning as yellow as the headlights of the trucks.

A hitchhiker walks a way, stops, and lifts his thumb.

In the desk are expired leases, snapshots, the stubs of all the checks he ever filled out. A snapshot of a smooth-haired terrier named: ?

The seasons keep on the move, like our feathered friends, the birds.

STARLINGS

The starlings are singing!

You could call it singing.

At any rate, they *are* starlings.

FRAGMENT (THE WHEELING SEASONS TURN)

The wheeling seasons turn
summers burn
then fall all fallow
in ripe yellow

The window looks over an arbor. The grape leaves, bluish green on one side and creamy on the other, are tossing every which way like a choppy sea churning up sand. Beside the arbor are four very tall hollyhocks, three with pink flowers, and one with red, like girls walking on a beach when the water is too rough for swimming. The hollyhocks sway in the wind like the masts of little sailboats, while the great elms and honey locusts bend as though they were underwater, with surf continually streaming through their upper branches. The sky and the river are the color of pewter, but the sky has been rubbed soft while the river is rough as ground glass. River and sky are kept apart by the hills on the farther shore, dark and muted, with buildings glowing in them.

The dense air brings the sound of a far-off train very close. Some orange daylilies are looking out from under the edge of the woods. They are not moving at all. The rain begins with a thousand pinpricks and a big yellow butterfly flying wildly about over the hedges, then stops. Bumblebees, like little flying bears, are floating up and down the stalks of the hollyhocks as smoothly as elevators.

THE TIMES: A COLLAGE

I'm not doing anybody
any good with my ideas

Buttering your face won't help

Jacqueline Cochran
saw the connection

Shall we be able to hold her
and study her as a fixed star?

Her only complaint in the past few weeks
is that she has had too much to eat

SNOW

Falling out of gray
on a schoolroom day
beyond the window.
A whisper: look, snow.

More gray fantasy
after a movie.
Snow falling at night
around a streetlight.

Thrown in shovel-loads
from walks, drives, and roads,
blown back in smooth drifts
snow shows how wind shifts.

THE BRIDEGROOM'S SONG

A notebook of white unlined pages,
My bride was mine, mine were the writing hands.

Riffling the fresh white many pages
My hands wrote history, my bride's and mine,
Drew curtaining words down each blind future page.

My writing hands wrote words, the same words,
            my hands stopped writing.
My bride is like a house with drawn curtains.

ADDRESS

Right hand graced with writing,
my left arm my secondhand new
suit bestrode, from the auto I
say, "Antinous, perched like a
parakeet cracking sunflower seeds
in a hot ice cave or cage,
you're an apogee. Acid pennies
will fill your mouth, your head
bowl at a soldiers' revel. Fly
the safety you despise and seek,
a butcher with a butcher's knife
peers. The lice are fast. Ta ta."

SWEET ROMANIAN TONGUE

Drew down the curse of heaven on her umbrella
furled and smelling of wet cigarettes,
Jo ran off in rain one pitchy night,
one bloody a.m. found her staring, snoring.

"Why do we all stay up so late?" Jo queried.
"Though I don't stay up so late as my friends."
She tripped the little bomb of wasps.
They got her.

Tears for Jo, four, each perfect, waspish.
A silver tongue and piss-blond hair
decants a funeral oblation for the mouse.

"She was a rare sight, a winning wonder.
Jo cultivates her toothaches elsewhere."

MISS WEEVY: WILL SHE MAKE OUT ALL RIGHT?

Five lanterns in her moon room
strung at different lengths, tonight
a Count to dine (flawless English!)
O daughter of Tidewater, so far
from home, is Rome her home? Yet here
she is: New York. Miss Weevy loves
love (who wouldn't when a taste of it
begets what a taste for more?), also
music, musicians, musical soirées,
all such tidbits as polar explorers
eschew, or is love other than a place,
faces, climates, a time? Seated beneath
her lanterns serving drinks, repines—
"O Italy was sunlight on a stone"
and something more, and more to be,
as she unstrings a night in manic laughs,
laughs to choose as she would be chosen.
Let love seal Miss Weevy's lips with its like:
a gold seal on a white tissue package.

DISTRACTION: AN ODE

Quale in notte solinga . . . —Leopardi

It clears away: the rain
is only rain that didn't fall.
I got my hair cut.
The night, well it's another
windy mess. In Andy's,
a stranger says he's got to use the phone.
"What's the emergency, jack?" says Andy,
and "If it's a baby, then the call's on me."
That's Andy. Tomorrow's Thanksgiving.
November is my birth month:
Indian summer, early dark,
sometimes snow. Were Andy's folks
from Naples? and what Andy
said was lipstick, and I thought was a scratch
on the stranger's cheek:
did his wife, when she felt her labor start,
fling out her arms?
Or was that phone call just a gag
like Andy says? Who knows.

Leopardi,
who would not believe
what you could not believe,
I love you so!
I will not go
to Recanati, when and if I can.
If it tortured you with boredom,
I believe you.
I've seen those hick burgs.
Still, "the sea, far off there . . ."
furrowed at dawn by a static ripple

the sea, the seafood,
the rabbit-warren streets
full of kids and junk and things to eat,
the grinning pushing lying thieving mob:
old No-Nose in the Via Chiaia
waiting to pounce: "She thinks I'm rich,
I know I'm poor; O.K., sister,
if you can take it, I can:
what's a penny between friends?"
the postwar gala
at San Carlo: the fatties
in their homemade-looking silks and black-and-whites,
Caniglia sang *Norma*
and her song
came up to me the way a line can fill a space
and sick with vertigo I looked down
on her fire-flashing wig:
Neapolitans can be very nice,
but Naples is not nice
that brought you—what's a wheezing cripple
among friends?—distraction
in human company.

Five years ago this winter
I wrote a letter,
something about the iron cold
and going out into a New York street
at night, the iron shadows of the el,
now gone, and high—
no one was in the street but I—
between skyscrapers leaning back,
ice-white, opaque,
the full sphere of the moon:
what did it mean?
I asked. That letter

I would redirect to you, long gone
into your naked grave.

Since, into how many graves
habitual stupidity has hustled
how many youths,
how many tears
have fallen and will fall:
so much in store.
Yet still the moon you sang
in the last song you wrote
on that volcanic slope—
how like a New York street, except
instead of broom, behind our tenements
the ailanthus fans its leaves
and a breeze
trembles at times its ancient blossom—
could you from there
across the bay see Naples?—rises
in all its phases
and reflects
the burning splendor of the sun
with reason in icy whiteness.

BEAUTIFUL OUTLOOK

Passersby see it as prison, grave, or den
into which their fear of what they fear lurks there
could drive them. Within, the walls are hung with light
like any room, meals are punctual and time
speeds, goes slow, does not exist, to suit the need
of each victim of the other side of love.

Sick or not sick, many here, had there been love
to make where they came from better than a den,
would not have come here. "I'm not a nurse. In there,
he'll get professional care." In the sunlight
the childish laugh and trot and maunder. Bedtime,
and no one gives the approving kiss they need.

Some here know how hard it is to know which need
is real. Consumed by an appetite, distrusting love,
making decisions they never made, a den
is what they pace. Locks, bars, stone, fear, rage, and there
stands choice, the keeper who blocks and guards the light
from those who must solve what must be solved by time.

What heals and kills? What takes back what it gave? Time.
The sense of its passing governs every need
of those here who thought it bore them past the love
that seems to stand outside it. Life was a den,
a womb, a night, a shrinking safety. Out there,
the envied strangers worked and walked in sunlight.

One, a boy, kneels and prays to the morning light,
staring while the sun blackens the sky like time,
happy beyond hope of help because his need

exploded. Out of the sun God pours his love
and calls him "my Daniel in the lions' den."
Like a man in the moon, he sees God's face there.

Passersby, think how many men are in there,
this hospital like a prison, on whom the light
never again will fall shadowlessly. Time
will bring them freedom in a grave. What they need
and have, and cannot have, matters to you: love
locked the doors and barred the windows of this den.

A hospital is not a den. The men in there,
the sick, saw light shatter, heard the tick of time.
Each man had his ugly need, each deserved love.

UNNUMBERED WARD

And accustomed ungentle hands of two blue-uniformed attendants
wrap the patient in suffering's white bed gown
sewn with bright invisible emblems of virtues,
or pinned with them, as with fraternity pins, or mosaic pins,
meaning travel. Has he always only just arrived?
Really suffering, within and without his head
burn hot wires of pain: "I cannot bear this": and does,
and does the time and place outwardly expound
what is within? To be well, to wear new clothes,
to decimate his wage for a necktie, a scarf or gloves, love
"your magic spell" scabbed his fevered lips, lay
no cold cloths, though to be him bent on him
eyes of those called to selflessness, lonely for more selfish days.

The hospital elevator is very slow,
it stops at every floor. Finally,
four. You knock on the battered
metal door of Ward 4N. A nurse
unlocks it and you ask to see
your friend. "I don't know if
he can have visitors today. Sit
here." She vanishes. The shabby
room is all too familiar (I've
been there myself). Time passes.
"Got a light?" a patient asks.
The light is given. Someone is
running. It's my friend, saying
my name. I call to him: he doesn't
hear. He's trotting, all bent
over. Then he goes back: to his
bed, I suppose. "You see?" the
nurse says. "He can't have
visitors today." "Is there any
point in my coming back to-
morrow?" "You might. He might
snap out of it." She unlocks
the metal door. That damned
elevator takes forever. In
the street it's hot and humid
and I sweat, and people walk
freely, going about their business.

GIFTS

for Lena Hartl

You are so kind
I will give you a little white horse
a child to mind
an apple for the little white horse
the child can give
flowers and fruit and a white sailboat
a place to live
for the child the horse the white sailboat
early lilacs
white as pearls hiding on white paper
a city park
hiding on a sheet of white paper
lilac people
St. Francis homespun and white roses
naked people
lilac and white as light on roses
you were so kind
when you showed me light at its quick source

ST. VALENTINE

Most of us misconceive saintliness.
It is easy to do.
If birds came to carry our messages
could we say it briefly?
Prisons imagine they wait to give us a refinement
hospitals missed.

An odd day to go look at pictures.
Odder not to have gone.

GROUSSET'S CHINA (*OR* SLOGANS)

Of course Tu Fu knew whom he sang to about beauty, sex and power:

>> they killed her on the far frontier
>> between capitol and capitol
>>> *douce et tendre*

Paintings, too, exercise the senses,
an Albers, white between pale yellow, pale gray,
singing as though nipples under matted March grass sighed for spring,
receptive, fecund with a nearly inaudible clear tone,
transparent as fraying mist in Cat King

Dubuffets that smell of germicidal liquid soap polluted with pine
blend an effluvia of urinals and wool
sur la plage, sur la plage

Kline's *Siegfried* and *Requiem*
> the bus a fat and leaping Greyhound
winds down on beaded Scranton, and in the station Wagner lifts the roof
> off, what has *muzak* come to, in the Polish Pennsylvania night?
> Take an elevator to the black coal corridors and see

Freilichers that entice like chubby roses and sleek banana leaves
under the trade wind–scoured sky a Vend-O-Mat says TACOS
a Schwitters (cherries and blue) essence of Ajaccio violets toilet-water
> after Barbasol
(Some people can't look at chicken wire without thinking
of flower arrangements, crumpled chicken wire is a swell flower holder
(household hint))

Goldberg, raw and suave, laughs cacophonously at the macaronis
pronouncing Billie Holiday: *vraiment, elle n'est pas artiste*

the French forties
and doesn't Giacometti make you want to slip an Ingres girl a feel?
or *La Source*'s navel make you think of salt and celery?
We will lift our thoughts higher. Now they are very high
up to the dandruff line in the wildroot-scented air
with a big-orbed de Kooning *Woman*, Miss Orange Crush, whose
                              eyelids come in three flavors
and in the window of course it isn't a window but smell in the night
blue snow and stars shooting roots
a precision of multiplicity

                        in a dark house sleep is sweetened by the Reinhardt
past passage of a new broom indistinguishable from air and silence
                     sleep knows as your nose knows aired linen
And if Brancusi made marble cry
              "don't touch, just you
                    kiss me"

and cursed Despiau, still:
those lustrous bronzes you might go dancing cheek-to-cheek with—
Step down.
I want to think about Niles Spencer's factory buildings
and a well-packed lunch box. Sandwiches wrapped in wax paper.
Hot coffee. An apple. Not a Delicious. A crisp yellow with flawed skin.

CONTINUOUS POEM

make it up

          irritability, hello

itchy and smeared

          April again

sparks blossom

          a lot to do

put these photographs away

          one two three four

this one no
tenements' swag
a square inch of it

          a bedsheet
          tacked across a window

a painter lives here
diffusing the light

          a rash breaks out
          on the park

pigeon-whitened

          fire escapes a
          winter's worth

scrub 'em
let 'em start fresh

      "Say, you have tears on your window"
      "That's paint"

TEARS, OILY TEARS . . .

Crying is a habit with me.
You mustn't mind: onions make me
smog
headlines in the *Daily News*,
not getting enough sleep
going to the movies and not going.
Fear of getting bawled out by people shorter than me,
animals in zoos,
deserted buses late at night,
tear gas, hunger, frustration
sob
and, oh, yes,
superfluous lines of verse and great beauty
move me to tears,
sliding out of me like oil
out of an over-oiled electric fan

SCARLATTI

last night
locked in
the castle
of pride and
egotism
goes on two
legs
        Webern
orchestrated a
sky the clouds
move to a
bass
on
an instrument not
an oboe, gray
on light-gray in
blue and green
goes by
on glass
      .   Schoenberg
serenades with
a view through
to where
a girl
swings
her
body displaced
against the
pull of her
hands head-
high on the
ropes

                night
before the night
before last
unlocked the castle
of pride and
egotism
                bliss
clouds stand
and go by

DANDELIONS

Hooray
for a change
  I'm letting the sky
     stay as it is
  tomorrow the sun may come out
     besides what's wrong
  with gray
        you can almost pat it
  and shape it
        smoke and dulled
  lights hovering in it
like clay
       greasy as fleece
    with air in it
like light,
       with light in it
like air
    and a steeple
    more coppery
    green than a grass snake
cool to the touch
      as the March breath
    in the hairs on my
arm by an open window
languidly snakes more or less now
drag themselves up on warm stones
among snow-faded matted fields
    and green shoots

SO THAT'S WHY

for Alvin Novak

Today—look at it—
It might as well be L.A.
with smog off the cold Pacific

but that posthumous *étude*
I bet you know he loved Bach!
don't you hear it when you
              play it and doesn't it
not surprise you? Maybe that's all
I had to say, remind
you how long the free Romantic line
is, how you've got it in your
wrists and fingers,

after all, the Clam Broth House
is pretty classical too:
it's hell after a storm,
when there's sand in the clams:

the music said more to me than that,
you see what makes me sick is
you can't just say

                    Chopin

and leave it in the air
like an unfrosted Mazda lightbulb
burning: someone will want to put a muffler
around it or a pleated paper shade
it's fantastic how people don't love beauty
yet you love Hoboken

                      Is that what
sort of regularly spaced sounds
you hear late at night?
                      (what a huge room you live in
and the Hudson instead of a pet dog,
                instead of a garden,
the tip of Manhattan, what a tip!)
say
                  so that's why you look
at a portrait of Chopin, so he won't seem small
and legendary,
        great, alive, different than us,
but different how? making notes on paper
        like Bach except
who could it be?

Chopin
                Here is his portrait by Delacroix
and it wouldn't look the same
if your left hand were not as strong as your right

of course the pianoforte is the triumph of civilization!

then you played
one of the *Songs Without Words*

TWILIGHT, WEST NEW YORK

Put her tits back, boys, we're coming into town.
The sky sweats, massaging a banker's bottom cloud.
The sun goes out like a butt in a urinal.
The hot star crotch prepares to spread its thighs
as a bird's crap flushes an overflow
down the Main Street false fronts.
Smoke it like a cigarette, don't chew it like a cigar.

EL MÉDICO

You're so young
already a doctor for how many years?
It's frightening
a European education
setting out knowing
nine out of ten will fail   is it the old idea of an élite
that sounds Spanish
it's more than that
it's a fact you're a marvelous doctor
all in white like a millionaire
all the same no wonder you have nine scars on you:
the stabbing the cancer
no wonder you went wild in Morocco and lost your rank
imagine getting *that* drunk
I imagine it quite easily
a month and a half in prison   that's another sort of scar
prisons at best aren't much
a castle not in Spain in Spanish Morocco
castles in Spain
of course are for romance
I won't ask again about Lorca   you were only five
the last time he came to your family's house
in Granada
what I can't get over
as a matter of fact
is the two extra days it took driving to San Sebastián
because of Madrid
it just never occurred to me that between 1936 and '39
anybody got into a car and drove from Granada to San Sebastián
you hated it anyway
it's a bore like Santander

you bet I'd like Torremolinos, Málaga and Seville
the world is for vacations it's a shame it isn't
                    you're twenty-six
today and spend your birthday far or not so far
from Madrid writing a paper about a new skin disease
                    except I get it all wrong
what's new isn't the disease, in this case, it's never been differentiated
                    before, is that it? Knock it off,
it's your birthday, we'll have a drink
                    or three, or four
                              felicidades, guapo

TO JORGE IN SICKNESS

You are sick in a hotel in Norfolk;
the weather there is fine: full of medicine and fever,
you may drive to a beach and I suppose walk on it.
Here, it has rained for three days.
The day is cold and opaline. It is Sunday.
I will bathe, dress and go see my friend John.
As I told you, we are writing something together.
I have so much to do. Most won't get done:
"first things first" "there are just so many hours to a day"
and I miss you
and am worried
"you must bundle up warm" "not overdo"
and I think how I might be there walking on a beach with you
in gauzy light and the medicated smell of the ocean
on the shadows of gulls
sliding silently on the sand as love
goes from us like a bird-shadow, or a desire for flight:

for my dual emotion
is to walk with you there in sunlight, which is love,
and to fly not from here but myself, which is childish.
Childish I am, you know, but if it is I you at all love,
let me wish what in my emotion is not childlike but childish
away and play at patiently
waiting your getting better and coming back.
Here the weather is ugly and smoky.
There the weather is clear and fine.
We talked on Sunday on an extravagant invention,
the telephone: I miss you.
Beware of bone-tiredness
that brings sickness.

JORGE PRONOUNCED GEORGE

Went South. We see him leaving
The Hotel Wade Hampton Columbia S.C.,
driving his very, very black car humming
"la dernier diamante" from
Massenet's *Manon* and arriving at
The Hotel Monticello Norfolk VA.
So many singles with showers and long distance phone calls!
So that is what life is about.

Jorge has trod on some toes.
Jorge wants to be able to go to the opera when he wants to.
Jorge wants a nice house
and has one.
Jorge wants to have friends
and has them.
Jorge doesn't want to be hurt anymore.
Jorge dislikes "marginal bohemian living" because it is sentimental.
Jorge is sentimental, in love, will be hurt.
So that is what life is about.

What a sweet dear good boy he is, I said aloud to the empty room.
I never expected to feel like Elizabeth Barrett Browning again, not this
    soon.
It's not so soon.
Surely it's undignified for a gent to want to take another gent
    bouquets, and absurd?
Just as surely I could not care less.
Surely it's an incredible invasion of someone else's privacy to sit
    around writing unsolicited poems to and about him?
Well, as you-know-who would say,
I'm sorry but I just can't help it I feel this way.
Deeply.
What kind of thing does a man say to a man he's in love with?
Things like, I can't tell you how adorable you looked in your new suit
    and that tie the other night.
Then he says, That suit is rather me isn't it,
then I say, Yes,
and the world lights up like the hot star they say it used to be
or may become,
burnt by the sun.
It's still glowing!
That's not my sleeve, that's my heart.
Not less than any other lover who ever wrote I want to describe
his looks, the way his wide eyebrows uniquely die away in a haze of
    fine short hairs on the east and west slopes of his forehead,
the way they join in a tuft, a small explosion of longer hairs above his
    nose, the crinkled pink of a new small scar, still touched by the
    black recent stitches,
the fullness of his lower lip, like the excess that shaped the pear, sulky
    and determined, boyish and sweet,
Greek, before they got refined:

but if I'm such a lover why can't I remember the color of his eyes?
I know their movements, how they twinkle wickedly (love is all about
    clichés)
when he's silly-drunk and cute,
how animal and slitty they get when he's tired,
their hard look at the floor when he won't be shy:
I think they're the color of the sky, which is not always blue.
Then there's his jaw that has a longbow curve to it
his hair curling on his nape, not silky or wiry, lively,
and in a quick transition to a longer view
the thin-skinned very naked whiteness of his back with muscles
    lapped and moving in it,
his belly, firm as a flank, sprouting little curves like dune grass around
    the Lake Nemi of his navel:
Moon! look down and see the small dark pit of your reflection on this
    pale shaded plain of flesh.
Heart, dream no further:
do you want to go off like the rockets on the Fourth at the Washington
    Monument?
I must get back to work,
but first I'll look at the clock and imagine where he is.

POEM (I FEEL I KNOW YOU VERY WELL)

I feel I know you very well
your favorite song I bet
is *Bill*

acute but wrong
I haven't got a favorite song
Then how about this
Under blue freeway lights

Driving to a big beat
headed for Bigburg
in a car with a bar
and a stereo tape
real late at night
with death at the wheel
under blue freeway lights

Driving from no place
headed for nowhere
with an unreal redhead
black at the roots
and if there's no gun
in the glove compartment
there's one at the wheel
spinning through a shadowless night

Not dead on arrival
not for want of driving (trying)
shot like a bullet
through the neon night

A YELLOW SONNET (INCOMPLETE)

thinking sunny thoughts of my sunny boy
on my desk a piece of yellow paper
reminds me that on Tuesday we will enjoy
each other in a tower whose top
sees all Manhattan as it seeks the skip of
a yellow square of sunlight on the floor.

I ASKED

I asked the wind the time
it brought me bells
such are our miracles.

I took the dishes out of my heart
and set the table places
with them with other dishes from hearts
interesting me no more than mine them.
Sleep brought me its undesired attentions
("Feign indifference if you would be loved
by your beloved," I read in a book
I wrote and burned and wish I had back,
that the wind with its bells took)
and lay upon me so I breathed painfully
and thought, "Who loves, suffers gladly,"
and, "I hate my suffering kind of love."

I want to take my dishes to a stream and wash them.
I will wear my overcoat and a green silk square and gloves.
I will sing songs we learned at school
and my dishes will float and sing among rocks
to become houses for trout. I will come home.
It will be as before, for who wishes the love
in his heart to die lives in terror of its death.

Zug.
Zumph. These words

out of a funnies.
What do the funnies say?

Look, in this drawing
they are walking up a country road
far from a great war.
The balloon coming out of the little one's mouth
says, "My, I'm sure hungry
and tired from walking."
The big one's balloon says,
"We can ask at that farmhouse up ahead
to put us up for the night."
Here, in this long panel that takes the space of three ordinary panels,
they are sitting around the supper table
with the farmer and family
eating creamed chicken on waffles.

VISITING THE KRESS COLLECTION

silk on silk
     I hate it
     I love it
     or don't give a damn about it,
a blond wintry flush in June.

     change the weather,
a child comes out of an orchard
in a tartan raincoat too big for her,
stomping in the wet.
           Queen Victoria
picking the spot for Balmoral,
         she doesn't know
there ever was a Q.V.
         why should she?
         Is history
an entertaining fakery?

on the phone
           "fifteen hundred dollars"
or "fifteen hundred years old?"
           ". . . fellow he said . . ."
what am I thinking about,
           you can't date Mayan
back   ". . . you fly to Manchester . . ."
fifteen hundred: little figures
           modeled in the round
priests   "Salem"
fantastically alive, like the football team
           ". . . if you get a great big
           free moment . . ."
from the Tonawanda Reservation
           ". . . holler. We'll get together and . . ."
hipless and fast. ". . . yik-yak."
           One priest is sitting on an altar.
He is rubbed with blue. "There's a case,"
           the dealer said, "a young
fellow with cancer of the brain.
           Six months to live."
They rubbed themselves with blue,
           with ointments and blood.

ACE BULLCATCHER: A COLLAGE

The picture expresses the squalor of modern loneliness:
flowers, clouds, houses, fishes, feathers, skies, street
corners, moths, fans,
abandon lucid mental control and free fancy.
1953
1933
1951
1896
1926 and 1927
1927
1919
1919 to 1925 with its disputes about the arbitrary and
the absurd still life with bread

★ ★ ★ ★ ★

He already knew all about the general trends
querulous and equivocal to the past
(living, spontaneous, lively, local)
clear and bright and the browns, grays, purple and cold
blues vie
suspended over an invisible abyss and with a vague sense
of guilt and anguish—
"Let's sit down and see if we can get anything done in
the next fifteen minutes without seventeen people asking me
questions!"—
and then ended the experiments of all that period
desolate and icily alone.

HORTENSE, THE CAPPADOCIAN TROGLODYTE

(Scene: Hortense's whitewashed cave in Cappadocia. A low door, a slot window through which sunlight streams. The cave is very clean, and Hortense, in a monk's habit, is somewhat not. A twig broom, a prie-dieu, a pallet. A plate of prickly pears on a bench.)

No one prays twenty-four hours a day every day. I know. I've tried. This time of year in Paris, the atmosphere is like an expensive scarf around the shoulders of a woman who passes through the rain from the theater to her equipage, the night pungent with slaves' cries and torch smoke. Though in Rome it is more like peeling an orange with a small knife, or biting one of those hard apples only goats and gourmets value. Evil cities, evil times. I followed the mob to the Basilica and heard Lecto preach. His offensive popular manner! As an imprisoned gambler will bet against himself on the racing roaches, the mob that lusts for entertainment converts the church to an annex of theaters until, single-mindedly, music lovers sense a truer worship in an evening swooned at the feet of some expert lyre banger than a morning crouched beneath Lecto's pulpit who excites the sense he excoriates. The sexy heave of breasts from which women tore brooches, beads, chatelains at his, "horrors of hell, o the black and fiery endless night . . ." But who can judge the purity of intention of an act?

DIM DIVERSIONS THAT OCCASION AN EXERCISE IN PURE THOUGHT LOGICAL, CONCLUSIVE, UNDEMONSTRABLE

Persons trivial to history, squalid enigmas usurping star
parts though scarcely featured players in what was not a pageant,
dim diversions to an exercise in pure speculation
and undemonstrable conclusion "based on a fresh assessment of
contemporary sources"—did the Dauphin die in
the Temple? A new theory, overpowering in its cogency—
Were the Casket Letters forged?—"and how about the *Marie Celeste?*"—
make their appeal by appearing in the guise of gods: personifying
forces, fears, desires, the unknowable about the known, the wish to
be famous, to vanish and punish, to be a public person but in
private. The veiled lady has a story to tell: haven't you, old tree,
new house? Coincidence in a name, the glamour and cash of crime
without the blood and reparation. Or to be greatness's sexy secret—
whether the object or the wish—to be purely a thought! Or a clay foot.
And who isn't in some way the estranged, the wildman without a wood?
Or dreamt a Minnesota or the warm smell of midnight
under the ripe grapes and just the sound of an ambling horse
comes over the wall. And had Amy looked before she stepped
"things might have turned out very differently from what in fact they did"
says Norman F. Cantor of Brandeis University.

A HEAVY BOREDOM

Not the light chiffony kind that lets you reach for a book
any book, the I-am-heavier-than-thou
sort that turns even Proust to dust and ashes

Electricity stirs the air
dust settles everywhere
I had sooner go bare

than sit pent in a business suit
Oh how this chafing burrs me!
not even Johnson's Baby Powder
soothes: my soles are creased and my pits
cranky and damp and sticky.

For is summer come
the lucky ones are sportive, from Maine to Key West
I like Southampton best
or perhaps a tourmaline lake like a tear in the heart of Vermont.

Too many skeeters. Scribble,
the tunes grow thin,
won't winter come, Coppelia?

TURANDOT

Perhaps the snow dragon picked out in crimson, or a pongee
sleeve scratched impatiently on the stone. You would not have known
our princess, and when the unattainable spends itself—like wishing
for a lot of money, and getting it—one might not know oneself. Her
future featured itself plainly as the plain across which, in the dawn
spray, a courier's pony gathered its little hooves. Whatever it is, it is
not enough, weighing more on her, our Turandot, than those stone
hairpins. She would despise to rehearse the gesture. Dreams
foreshadow, and very still on the battlement below the archer's feet
who cannot look, if her lips shaped a word, why should it not be,
Japan? or, America!

FANFARE ON A DOG-VIOLIN

John Ashbery is understood to have passed
in a way of his own, en route to one
of the emblematic neckery shops he favors.
He is said to have been about to
exchange a flowery crepe for a chaster ice-
blue satin number, or to telephone the folks
at Sodus, New York, near the fire-gray
water of Lake Ontario, reputedly his
favorite lake. When he comes back to us
we will advance in a chorus chanting,
"Thank you John Ashbery for coming to
see us so we see you in new clothes.
We always have loved you and admired your ties."
That is how we feel about John Ashbery.
Here he comes now. I will thank him personally for
"the salacious paperbound books and girlie magazines."

"DEDICATED TO G. VERDI. BECAUSE IT'S HIS BIRTHDAY."

Good afternoon, John in Paris. Can you hear
your city station by transatlantic phone?
"This one or that." Of course I don't know who the tenor is.
Since I forgot your birthday
this July this seemed an apt excuse
to phone. Or haven't you a phone at 14, Rue Alfred Durand-Claye
O sage of the Rue Alfred Durand-Claye?
All that's different since you left
is the widening crack above your bed.
They're not taking this building down a minute too soon.
And a beige monster with an air-conditioner duct
under each aluminum casement blocks what was a view.
Sometimes I feel like I just dropped in here
to say goodbye. It takes a heap of leaving
to get a house condemned, I reflected
reading Van Vechten's *Parties* (again, for heaven's sake)
recollecting
how Hal broke his arm on the steep stairs.
You typing at your desk, a letter for a map-lined
envelope, or reading *La Modification*
explicating Pixérécourt. Jane's portrait still is fresh
though dusty. I just unearthed Frank's
copy of F. T. Prince's *Poems*. Dated Ann Arbor.
Oh dear.
I wish you were here. I'm feeling rather like Leopardi said,
Don't wish your Saturdays to haste away.
They will anyway,
                    Lina Pagliughi
is about to sing "Caro nome." It's enough to break your heart

"Daddy! why are you upset?"
"It's that vile damned race of courtiers.
   Don't talk to men in church."
Without the phonograph and the radio,
what has the twentieth century to offer?
The *National Geographic*. Remember to send
the article I clipped for you on glider flying
in '31 in Germany. Or maybe '30. This phone call
into the fond void of international airmail
(the flautist is fluting on a pre-Columbian
ocarina I think)—*Acquapendente*—
            aren't you tickled by place names
that only rustle up a stop for dinner in the rain?
Like a Spirit of '76 spot
that means a leak and coffee in a Greyhound post house.
The hero sandwiches north of Boston,
a liberal helping of
The Great Atlantic & Pacific Tea Company
mixed salad on salami. . . . "Cara nome"
lacks a bit of the old Red Seal magic
of Galli-Curci. It livens up when the hunchback
cusses out the gang. I wish it were raining
on the Boulevard de Sébastopol and I, squelching
along, mildly certain to encounter you—
for an instructive stroll. I wonder what became
of Mealy Potatoes? Write
or phone.

LETTER POEM TO KENNETH KOCH

Dear Thunderbird,
Letters should be confidential but I've no confidences
so might as well write you a poem in the new form
only the initiate can tell from prose. Hello.
Hello Kenneth. Hello Janice. Hello Katherine. So you can scream like
power brakes. I hear from the Moustache by way of Jane. Grand.
It's "fragrant May" (Leopardi)
(I'm typing in a pool of my own sweat)
and New York is blindingly beautiful
thanks to the aluminum people
who are not cast of Canadian metal—they have weekend
sunburns and suits bluer than heaven you can wash in the sink
yourself, even as you and I. What they got
we haven't got is a lot of aluminum.
You run up some beams and snap
the aluminum whosies into place
and glass—sparkle! toward sundown
going east you have to walk horizontal. Except
the House of Seagram, austere and smoky
as a molten topaz. And now for personalities on parade,
while vending Picasso catalogues at MoMA
—that haven of have-not poets, I heard a guard say . . .

LE WEEKEND

1
It must be very confusing to be named John.
It is not an uncommon name like Snedens Landing.
It is an even more common name than Arthur,
Though it may not seem so to Bobby,
Living as he does, flanked by men named Arthur.
If this is confusing, blame Jimmy.

Is it hard to be hard on someone as nice as Jimmy?
No, it is not. Ask John.
Imagine: those two snoozing at Snedens Landing!
It must have appalled early-bird Arthur
who slept later than Bobby
who was in the kitchen, baking a cake with Arthur.

On the frosting of the cake they wrote, "Arthur,"
in icing, then gave the pan for "licks" to Jimmy,
because he is greedier than John,
the second-greediest person ever to visit Snedens Landing.
"Is it my birthday?" mused Arthur
when he found the cake, hidden so carefully by Bobby.

2
"If you don't know, who does?" said Bobby
from behind the cake tin, where he was lying in wait for Arthur;
bumpety-bump-crash, down the stairs fell Jimmy.
Was this a diversion? Or had he been shoved by John?
Or by the infamous ghost of the grapes that haunts Snedens Landing?
Down from the room stumbled Arthur.

"Did I mean to peek?" cried Arthur.
"Bring my medicine chest," caroled Bobby.

"I made it into a shadow box," chuckled Arthur.
Malingering on the floor lay Jimmy
waiting his chance to bite John.
These are common occurrences at Snedens Landing.

There is nothing common about Snedens Landing.
How could there be, with its river view designed by Arthur,
its kitchen supervised by master chef Bobby,
its musicales arranged by tasteful Arthur?
Its uniqueness is affirmed by the ubiquitous Jimmy.
It is sustained by such visitors as the champ croquet pro John.

We have gone with John on a visit to Snedens Landing.
We have met Arthur and learned from Bobby
there is more than one Arthur. Nor did we escape meeting Jimmy.

KENNEXTH

1

Lemon village with walk foot gorilla
burnished Miss Thirst. The. And. Tea
have are drunken look shop China
uncups, is hunting Jane-John for eat Grace-hoops
honey-money bee-haven happy-un-bee
wear winter season summer light lice Kennexth.

2

"Isn't is gnats midges, sorry Kennexth,"
Oh un-city club berry milk gorilla!
Fashion'd of silver lama pot plant tea.
They drink. It. And. The. China
velly big, belly old, rope quoit hoop
O Cincinnati! plowed under Rome bee

3

hive, first Latin year Kennexth bee
(K-harp, K-hats, K-ha-ha-hatree Kennexth!)
hero eat-branch, heat bunch gorilla
bar-belle glass lifter fan in tea
smoke. More parties, O my chin-chin china
chow dog for graceless dinner bong hoop—

4

ful, -less, -ly, bowls Venice hoop
regular follow felon "brute of a bee"
snout auto quarrel pet-bug valley Kennexth.
"You are my diamond mine gorilla
girl. Strew the brewn pot sew tea
leaves. I love strew." China

5

never more my "moor," un-tin, my knot-China.
cursed electric blanket chinafying the gift hoop
when Frank O'Hara charlestons in charleston bee
s be happy for the tyke. Him dance. Him Kennexth
send sanka card, Santa paws. Embraceable toy gorilla
boy, for cage grown age hair-nipple, sieve rich tea.

6

The hand of the night emptied a pot of rich tea
in a wind-row beet sugar caper bush China
plan-tu-tation. It is not as un-not as it is hoop.
Our hope, my hop, your hip. I kist the bee,
I devoured lunch-wise yatch-crawl bee-bee gun Kennexth
brought—O Tibet orange lemon sun! in arm-gorilla
panda baby home home white-pink bath milk, are these tears tea?

A gorilla we see in an extra line of tea
unvitrifying a china cup-saucer hoop
from which June Bee drinks secret Kennexth.

VARIATIONS

1

    lilac
    dandelion
    curve
    sublime moment
    trench coat
    gorilla

2

Between lilac storm clouds
we briefly see the dandelion sun
and the clouds sway shut
as lilacs heavy with rain curve
over the drive, each weighing drop
as it falls a sublime moment.
Storm clouds unseasonably lilac,
in its autumnal trench coat
the earth resembles a gorilla.

3

Flowers and shrubs, clothes, animals and time,
perforce in all we find definitions of curve.

4

That a man all animal clothed in hair
should curve his arm and fill the crook
with boughs of lilac ripped from the shrub
with his delicate dark-palmed hand
that picked the juicy hollow-stemmed dandelions
to wear in his trench coat when he danced.
Gorilla, clothing sublime moments with flowers.

5
Green hearts, is blue and pink
seen in heap on heap
of bundles of cones
of waxy birthday-cake candleholders
truly called lilac?

6
Coat of certain cut,
planting bulbs in a trench,
we found bones.

7
Sublime, pertaining somehow to heights,
like summit, though at the summit
of certain moments
we touched sublime depths.

8
Who came so early
we save for last,
darling blondes,
little suns,
breezy snowtops,
acrid weeds,
buttering fields,
wild in domestic lawns.
Old women in the early rain
will gather you for a salad.

9
Down the drive hedged with lilac
and overgrown with dandelion
around the blind curve your sublime moment,
idling in your trench coat,
will be to see the sun's fist,
the fist in your way of a gorilla.

GARMENT

Unnerve me sir, trounced to a boneyard
bedded sheer gulley slide side. The raft
drifts nude space placed, ruddering bags
lousing creek creeper skimmers. Simmer
samovar, juicy steam unlooked love put
upon the put upon. You quarried of me
a nickel worth o' ore, O fool: scummed
water flow full, typhic, highway-viewed.
"Be back come dogwood and jay scream."
Go go go go go . . .
Reel wheels, roads, whippet, our car, a
way away. *Strasse* us Phoebus abedward,
nourish soft-shoulder flounce of Pennsy,
Mount Joy valley view. Thoughtfully sewn
of corrupt flesh the fair brittle hair,
willow twig dipt, babble toned, you go.

BIRDLAND (*OR* CALIGULA-CALIGULEE, *OR* COME INTO THE GARDEN MAUD, THE GRASS NEEDS MOWING)

NOIA: Now I am going to dance. I am going to dance a good long time. I am going to dance very slowly and clumsily. I am going to dance just as much as I please. It is going to be very boring for all you out there. I don't care. I am going to dance anyway.

CAPTIVE AUDIENCE: A-a-a-a-a-h!

VOICE FROM THE REAR: Take it off! Take it off!

(Enter the Goodman brothers with each other's heads on duraluminum platters. The swing duet from Messager's *Veronique* tunes in.)

CAPTIVE AUDIENCE: Kill that woman!

NOIA: I am still dancing! (And so dies Noia, Princess of Bavaria, crushed beneath the windshield of her own Thunderbird.)

As the curtain tenderly falls, the bird audience, released from its cage, twitters, *e pluribus unum* . . . *il mondo è fango* . . . *il faut tenter* . . . *nudus Amor formae non amat artificem* . . . *de cette nuit, Phénice* . . . *and waft her love* . . .

and the lights come up

SENTENCE (*OR* SENTENCES)

Stir them up and they won't stick.
The.
We will let you have our thinking on it timewise pronto.
Look at the nun. How greedy she is.
Alaska, nearer to Siberia . . .

It was considered fashionable about 1837.
Now it is out of date, outmoded, no longer stylish.
Still, she brings to it an air . . .

The place has run down since Gramp's day.
Alabama Beach, and Cat Cay, and Towser.

JUST AWAY (*OR* JONQUILS APPROACH)

Jenny sleeps
On the porch.
Her long lashes lie on her woolly cheeks.
Now she is dreaming of the rabbits of West 11th Street.

Ah,
Spring,
How soon you have gone, leaving us
Buttercups and the flowering potato fields of the Hamptons!
Even John
Regrets this heat,
Yearning, on dog days, for the coco locos of seaside Mexico.

J is for my name is Julia, J is for John and for Jane
U is who you are
L is easy to tell, it's for Liesel, and for love to talk
I is who I am:
A rather young Miss Gruen who on September two is two
                             And wishes you

A happy on my birthday,
                    Anne, Angelo, Arthur and all

G, going on three
R, the three I begin to learn
U-turn in at our new old house on Cobb Road
E of course is for Elizabeth
                    and I'm sorry there's no K for Kate
N, now is the end
          of my birthday song: a very happy on my birthday
             Joe-Jane, Chum, Fairfield, Bobby, Jenny, Jimmy and all

FAR OFF

For
Raunchy
And
Noli me Tangere,
Kyrie Eleison.

Out the window the UN Building shines
'til the sun sets. Then it's a gravestone in the dark.
Have
All the
Redskins run
Away? I'm blue!

A BLUE SHADOW PAINTING

for Fairfield

of an evening real as paint on canvas.
The kind that makes me ache to have the gift
for dusting off clichés:
not Make it new, but See it, hear it, freshly.
The context (good morrow, haven't we met in this context before?)
in which, squelch, a brush lifted a load
of pigment from the thick glass palette, and, concentrated,
as though he saw neither the work in hand nor the subject,
the painter began. A rapt away look, like a woman at the theater
who sorts laundry, makes a mental note, while the stars anguish,
to buy a bottle of Scuff-Coat tomorrow at Bohacks.
The painting is of a sloppy evening in a burst of daily joy:
at the left orange flames—were they bushes?—a black-gray tree,
at right, houses, buildings, no more there than, well,
two gray strokes together, casual as a scribble, make a slate-
roofed tower. Then there's one place where light pink came to rest
under a faded buttercup sky.
It's like this: the orange assertions, dark there-ness
of the tree, malleable steel-gray blueness of the ground; and sky;
set against, no, with, living with, existing alongside of and part of,
the helter-skelter of rust brown, of swift indecipherables. The day
is passing, is past: mutable and immutable, came to live
on a small oblong of stretched canvas. Blue shadowed day,
under a milk-of-flowers sky, you're a talisman, my Calais.

WATER LILIES

Once, after dinner, at Penobscot Bay,
the sun set in an inarduous and total
show, slowly or suddenly
it drew the water tightly
more rosaceous—petal-smooth and petal-colored,
petal-curving, like a brimming cup
at the edges of the rocky islets,
inwardly afire, a stemmy shine, harsh rose-leaf serrate.
Lichen rusted and with black spot
which were spruce, the sky,
the blues and greens precedent to deepest violet.
A painter said, if you saw it in a painting
you would hate it. A sculptor grunted his assent.
It's nice of Monet to have proved them wrong.

AUGUST 6TH

Now it is the strawberry leaves that are red
down among the wiry stalks of the grass
that bend their seed-shedding beards toward the south
where the brow of the meadow drops its obliquity
to the bay and seals that snort and vanish
and there are islands each profile
of jammed spruce or grass head on rock
with its own shadow individual as a name

AUGUST 22

It's hot today.
The black roofs are bright.
The sky is nearly white
it's so hot today.

On an island far away
are moss-grown steps
among birches and spruces
above a wind-wrinkled bay.

A canoe floats on the water
over bars
and devil's-apron,
a man and his daughter

take a paddle on the bay
in the time before supper.
I wish I were there
on that far-away bay.

Feverish and hot by night,
by day hot and bright,
city, though you have me,
you don't please me.

Goodbye, last blueberries,
fully ripe blackberries,
reddening cranberries,
fragrant bayberry.

Quick! I must get out of bed.
It is lunchtime. The rain
that never really got started
has stopped. We are leaving
the island and I must pack
the dry bouquet of lichened twigs,
water-worn glass and whelk and mussel shells
a gray-green stone and a sea-urchin—skeleton?—
green with white bumps and five-rayed, all
disheveled in a scallop shell. I must pack
the unbaked-cookie-shaped-
and-colored sand dollars that shake
with a dry click of a pre-tambourine,
a rock with two meshed veins
of quartz like crazy teeth,
the knobby lumps of white or liverish and faded
unsemiprecious coral and a crayon drawing
on a shingle of an angel and a heart
pierced by a green arrow and labeled
GOD IS GOOD. The other stones
may stay, along with the passionate blue
Bromo-Seltzer bottle vase.
Except this fat arrowhead-shaped stone
the color of red chocolate or raw liver
that was to be the, so to speak, cornerstone
of a vast collection of same-colored stones
from the stony Double Beaches.
I must pack the khaki pants
with the unpatched knee,
the letters,
the postcards from France,

the night-beguiling books from the New York Public Library,
this typewriter and its eraser.
O tides! O ocean swell!

SEPTEMBER SUMMER HOUSE

Out into the harbor mouth
sticks a rock blob
barred to shore by sea gunk
a bar stretched thin as pulled bubble gum
but it doesn't snap back.

On a quilt on the grass
that isn't grass
a baby jabbers
at his parents taking the sun
with them to New York.

Boats depart:
John Walton, Suzy Q,
Elizabeth A., Kittiewake II.
People arrive:
five: it seems a throng

on the float
a floor of an outdoor room.
Just that—the float—and it makes
walls and windows
of air, invisible, exact.

Wind lines lie on the water.
The baby barks
mimetically: a gull barks back
for avian reasons
of its own (raw-fish-eating bird logic).

A fly in the room
adds its buzz to that of those without

the house, old for its age:
wood, paper, glass,
some nails and metal fittings,

a few sticks of furniture,
some paint, some cloth,
some wood to burn
in the chill depths
of a red and yellow room.

POEM (A NOTHING DAY FULL OF)

A nothing day full of
wild beauty and the
timer pings. Roll up
the silvers of the bay
take down the clouds
sort the spruce and
send to laundry marked
more starch. Goodbye
golden- and silver-
rod, asters, bayberry
crisp in elegance and
small fish stream
by a river in water.

EVENING

A rabbit and a robin
hopping on the lumpy lawn

eating rotting cherries
and fallen mulberries

a rabbit with a jackknife kick
and a robin with a short neck.

nibble and peck,

fruit of which there was too much for us to eat
while we ate steak

UNTITLED

Our world slips on a silver sweater,
its head, fighting out of the tight neck,
now a blue sun, now a moon,
the pewter of pigeons. Not a bright blue sun,
a watered one, a yellow blue
that isn't green, rather, an oystery secretion
cold, gritty, and tasting of the sea.

Who would want a silver sweater?

The skyline is all brushwood,
chopped and set for sweetpea vines,
a likely story. The moon
this year is extra flat,
smooth and smelling strongly of bay rum.
The sun is extra small.

An unexpected change in weather
remarks,

> "Don't say, suppose, or think
>   what November will or won't be,
>   take it as it comes. You
>   have no choice."

The sky this almost-evening afternoon
is swamp water frozen
into wind-ridged ice out of which
stick bearded straws. (A big
four-footed beast runs, skids and falls
and lies there, lifting its

noble antlered head with a surprised
tricked look of a neophyte bike-riding child
who took a spill then frighteningly, thrashing,
finds its footing and is gone.) Then it
breaks up a bit
and shows a bright blue baby fist.

SOFT SAWDER SKIES

These early heavy frosts wash colors out
a horse eats a faded field
frost after frost and there's plenty of mulch
why should one shrub
have on some unturned leaves? Maybe
there's an intruder in the hedge

and two great trees
only seem to thrust toward each other
their twig-ending branches to
passionately interlace in the unsunniness

of today. Oh well, it's Monday,
no wonder things look washed out,
even the pup under the dining-room table
looks up with a hangdog look

Wet without rain, warmer but far from warm,
clouds boding snow though it won't—
no wind—tick-tick goes the little clock
when a whole day is like the pause
of someone sleeping, whose breathing
stops, or seems to—a sharp awakening
to another not-quite-asleep—well then,
sensations of breathlessness are bound to follow.

AFRICA! AFRICA!

A match clears the air, congestion
of the chapel organ tones family
circle faces. How we hate to love!
Nephew Noxious pops his teeth and
the nameless others fatly quiver.
Boredom's puffy toes kick us in
our Sunday-supper-swollen guts. I
flip my butterfly routine, sundry
as Monday wash. Hairpins detonate.
On the wall Christ refutes doctors,
germanically, divinity, come back,
fudge us again, us lost ladies
who heard a bullet, stop to answer
the craftiest command of inert man
rolled from the colossal ear. Year
of hell and harmony, spill you a
good sleep, near the zebra's hoof.

THANKSGIVING

The windows of Our Lady of Poland,
rich and big in a small church
a glow in frosty dead-elm-leaf-and-ocean-smelling evening,
sumptuous, like sumptuary laws,
which I hope regulate adornment
not restrict it.

November passes, quick as passing
the windows of Our Lady of Poland, from the station
to the house, in a wealth of saints' days:
best wishes, Lizzie, on St. Elizabeth the Queen's day:
the Bohemian glass bounded, unshattered,
down the rocks; best wishes, Kates,
although I confess, an American, I think
of brainy, young, lovely Catherine Wheels,
nailed to a tree, spiraling in the dusk.

There are no or few November flowers,
here, lilacs, after a hurricane,
bloomed and for my birthday weekend
Fairfield put robed, dark blossoms in an Eastern bowl
leaning by the guest-room bed,
four-posted: Matthew, Mark, Luke and John: without a tester,
except testy I. A few unseasonable branches of delight
in their heart-shaped leaves, between storm door and door
for Miss Kelly, whose view of miracles is reasonable
and strict. I agree (or like it both ways).

November, month of St. John of the Cross,
the saint it is easy to imagine patron
of poets: and if I am wrong, I am sorry

and grateful, recalling, a war ago,
walking along Third Avenue
with a small book of his poems, while trains roared.

November, month of St. Anne.
November, lilacs, pink-and-blue of lilac-colored lilacs, and white.
St. Elizabeth of Hungary.
St. Catherine of Alexandria.
St. John of the Cross.
St. Anne: in the calendar of saints
by the sink, a note about St. Joachim.

AN XMAS SCRIBBLE

Let mad applause greet the bearer of the cross,
"He's very good, he's learned our lesson,"
an Easter lily flame tips the Christmas trees
upon toy trains and ties, or fills your stocking
with a severed leg. The days pass like a spilling
of calling cards gone dusty on a card dish.
"This hall is filthy. Where are our servants?"
"Why should I have to keep my own house clean?"
To one and all in hospitals and prisons, cheer.

NEW YEAR

I wish I might
have heard Hortense Schneider.
No. I've had my
fair share. As Gertie says,
"Those shadows
on the window
are making
me blue."
Bill, dead of
leukemia, is alive
and we're in Florence
coming from a
Josephine Baker
sing-in. Perhaps he'll
bat me one again.
Facing forward, toward
death, it pleases me
here in a friend's home
to be drunk, to greet
the new year hearing
"Gertie"
sing
"Limehouse Blues."

We all lay on the island beach together,
now they are gone. Brian and his friend
the redhead, each dead of his own hand.
Leukemia took Bill. Wystan and Chester
passed on, as they say, in sleep. I bid
them adieu. The beach view, we say, was of
water and, winking into sight, the distant hills
that environ Naples, where the lurking beggar
was aptly known as No-Nose. She got the money
that she begged for. Brian was
an impossible man, an arrogant drunk. Bill
had high ideals he never could live up to.
Perhaps only Wystan was, in an angry way,
serene. Each face, not excepting mine,
was eroded by booze. We took a group
trip, I and the others, from an island
to an island and on to Sorrento, Amalfi,
Pompei and Naples and back to Forio. We
knew our way quite well. Now, except myself,
the sightseers are gone, dead and gone.
Good day, good night.

IMPROMPTU: DORABELLA'S DREAMS

What a sweetheart, openhanded Dorabella
takes friends on a European jaunt. Or is it
that white, deep-cuffed great-shawl-collared
robe, wistful at a Ritz window? Chopin,
champagne, rain. Dreams of giving it all
away, money that gets between one and one's
best friends. Life was so much more fun before
—well—before. Her nerves need the sun
and she needs a new bathing suit, and sandals
and now all the really fun people go to Lebanon
all the ones she met when everyone went ski-
ing in Spain. Or a Brazilian withdrawal?
Poor Dorabella, better to be insecure in these
insecure times, so people like one for oneself.

In the mountains of Spain
we gathered violets, you and I,
the pain, losing you. I
don't care, so you were tactless
to clerks! Castles toppled
at my big pink feet the day
of your note. Saint C.'s.
Monica, why? Don't answer.
Stay. Rain on the quai,
the Quai Voltaire isn't it?
I hate Paris, these meetings
in the Rue Scribe, posters
we laughed at: Frères Lissac.
Rain on plane trees: you
knew I went back to Albi?
Though I walked erect
they knew I kissed each
stone. The hotel manager
asked after you, spite-
ful, drunken Belgian. No.
I won't. I know I've no right
to touch. To touch you!
I ate you like bread. Your
silly name: Monica. Money.
Honey. Monica. "I'm not a
love-slave," you said. We
talked like that then, spit-
ting bitter coffee. Go
on, go. Get wet. It's your
dress, your life, you're
you. I'm I. Goodbye.

CHABRIER

The sky is like a grater.
The sun sets.
You can't see it.
The Airedales sleep,
each on its rug.
I knock the paper to the floor.
By accident. And then
I pick it up.
A real nature lover
I took my walk.
Rose hips red
as Gerhardi's lips.
And thought my thoughts
and planned my plans
and: "But he," I thought
"is another cup
of manure tea."
Some days, Firbank
laughed so hard he
couldn't go on writing.
I bet Chabrier was like that
too. Heart, overflowing
with grace, tenderness,
inventiveness and wit,
bless this coming year
for me, for one, for all.

LEONARDS LAKE

I took a walk to Leonards Lake one day
during the spell of beautiful weather.
I went once in the fall and noticed
the fall foliage and animals. This time
I noticed the winter scenery. I saw
and heard chickadees, heard evening grosbeaks
and saw seagulls on the ice on
Leonards Lake. I could see much further
than in the fall. When I got back
I painted pictures, trying to recall
the many different colors I observed
in the snow and ice. I tried to paint
Mrs. Clark's house across the lake. When
spring comes, I will go again and
notice how different things look.

FROM THE ISLAND

The hawsers of my life loosen: a tinny toot:
the goodbye boat.
By these sky-sutured spruce and that white distant sail,
though I go in fog on a black and bucking bay,
all winter will an island welter in my sight.

Dawn smites, storms, and the sea,
molten at dusk. Palm fronds crack,
heat, bougainvillea, wrenched brown
as amethysts, a sunstruck boy's
lipped-red neck. Scab in the sea,
we bussed to you and fans drove
a fluid welcome. Fear shook me,
sentry of the vast moon, heady
light and snake shadow. Who goes
there, goes unknowing of wet fire
etching raw itching creases, eyes
flung a dazzle down to sink jelly-
fish, the aquamarine zebra fish,
angelfish, hang. Barracuda by garbage
barge, would let blood, salt the
salt, like urine. One gold-earringed
effebo, crouched, leapt, laughed.
Spear the sea, frenzied, far cried
north ice-light's daughters for bone-
heat, sweat, rain, wind lash, stress-
ful of a cypress house. Dry moss,
hair of desert death, whisperer,
the condemned men laughed, sailed.

POEM (BETWEEN GLACIER AND GLACIER)

Between glacier and glacier
it is pleasant to stumble
or stand on big pebble beach
by a granite boulder a
rich citric lichen has grown
on into a map of
only itself so slowly year
after year so
quick between glaciers.
It is as tall as you
perhaps since you can't
quite make out its base
that might be tied in a tail
like a balloon so full
it slowly leaks
misshapenly. To the touch its
hardness, rough as a hand,
seems a shimmer of sand
after a while. The atoms
dance. In the bay
a curious seal rises
and dives and the spray
sparkles granitically.

HELEN'S WALK

Buried too many canaries, sprayed
for black spot too late too many roses,
unraked, unweeded, the gravel drive.
"There is Helen in the lime walk. How
slowly she walks! She looks very unhappy."

A bird-whited, rain-slimed birdbath,
a brittle vine, a dank garage ravaged
of tools except a sprung-toothed bamboo
lawn rake. In the ragweed beds, lupines.
An inchworm measures Helen's blouse.

THE HOME

The turrets, self-conscious and vulgar,
the doors, so functional,
the tinted windows, lovely and perhaps unreasonable.
It had a plan, it must've,
even if the plan were only to build it as it grew,
vulgar and lovely, a palace
that was also an office building, a slum, a factory,
an abandoned fun house near a dump.
They moved in and lived there.
They became like their palace
which was so like themselves before they moved there.
From the vulgar turrets,
watched many a presumed-to-be-functional movement
of the sun, or of clouds,
or of a wind pushing rain aside like bead curtains.

WELCOME

In the dining room in March,
the plain country dado
painted gray, with paper
patterned the pale colors
of the beech ·
beyond the end of the street.
And prints from Japan
faded as March.
At the window: a swing
swinging in the wind,
its seat a faint green,
less bright than moss green
on trunks of elms that arch
and stretch like someone
just out of bed. Invisible
buds, up the street, high
on the trees make a haze,
a flush, the way wind
brings blood to cheeks,
winter-pale, as here the earth,
eyes shut, tips back its head.

IRRITATION

Spring waltzed in today,
making dry eyes itch and burn.

Ornamental cherry trees
don't fruit,

just blossom
like squirting pigeons,

what spring
fever's like, each year.

Itchy and sticky
and half-dressed,

blinding reflections,
runny noses,

the world's a dusty
winter remnant.

APRIL

The morning sky is clouding up
and what is that tree,
dressed up in white? The fruit
tree, French pear. Sulphur-
yellow bees stud the forsythia
canes leaning down into the transfer
across the park. And trees in
skimpy flower bud suggest
the uses of paint thinner, so
fine the net they cast upon
the wind. Cross-pollination
is the order of the fragrant day.
That was yesterday: today is May,
not April and the magnolias
open their goblets up and
an unseen precipitation
fills them. A gray day in May.

JULY 3RD, 1975

At four a.m. the air conditioner's
gentle hum. I'm so glad I got
it: July, August, my two unfavorite
months. I hate it, heat that makes
me burn and peel (really, summer sun
is beautiful, flashing off tall stony
glass and metal buildings). I go
(it is the weekend of the Fourth)
this afternoon in mob scene to
cooler, green and white Southampton.
Why do I always whine and carry
on about the scorching weather?
Year in, year out. Fall is not that
far away: Vermont, and the turning
of the leaves.

HEROIC SHAPE

Then, in the asexual embrace of a summer
trolley (the conductor trailed his foot
swinging along the footboard: clink, clink:
dimes and tokens) it seemed under a boy's
beret you said about warming a cold snake.
How black you were in that white, white city.
Since, many springs flower-fruit the wisteria
on the passing wall, and lover's leap lost
its romance, but you, black, black, still
speak of the snake in sparks and clangings.

ON THE WAY TO TOWN

And so on the farmhouse porch we said goodbye
to our friends in the sour farm smell
and an ammonia drift from the cow barn
and we were free to drive away,
who have shared car seat and bed for many years,
therefore leaving me free to think
whether I like our friends, whether one can say
one likes anyone more than things,
or do things, places and plants, loved humanly
become mixed to us as persons?
Plants that won't bloom, the soil of a place gone sour
hurt us like a friend's betrayal?
Driving under clouds like water-rippled sand
broken into starlit places
with you whom I think I neither love nor hate
beside me, without whom my life
would have been different, but how, I don't know,
I pretend I like wild places
more than persons, without whom I could not live,
and so I turn to you who shares
your life with me, to ask which plants you like best.

POEM (AS I CAME BY THE SWIMMING POOL)

As I came by the swimming pool
with a cup of black coffee
I saw a copper-colored beetle
threshing its notched legs where the water
running into the pool makes a current.
I went on my way, then went back
and got the skimmer, a springy oblong
screen-on-a-handle used for skimming
leaves and dead bugs from the pool
and lifted the bug which clung
as soon as it was free of the water
to the screen, feigning dead.
I laid skimmer and bug on the burnt grass
and got my coffee and came in here.
So, I just saved a bug from drowning.
But if it had been a bumblebee,
well, twenty or so years ago
one lit on my neck and stung me.
It was in class, and, thinking it was a spit ball,
I tried to wipe it off.

POEM (THE SUN STANDS STILL A SEC)

The sun stands still a sec
to catch its breath and noon
comes out of the screened porch
in a wrapper which it takes off
to lie, naked, among and on
white plates that float on air
brown nipples and unlikely pubic
hair but likeable as the brown
reflected spruce and the sun in
bliss sighs in transparent heat.

TO J.A. IN PRISON

Lost my glasses
sun crap in my hand
brown weeds green
the green lightning
bald blue day
taken aghast:
"Am I the Empress of the waltz?"
Find and bind
answers to Bowser
say Uncle to Auntie
if sun rise like a face:
"Is Japan an island?
New York is"
dark park

JANE SCULPTS

Lookie lookie here comes Jane, and the kick
pleats of her Egyptian goddess gown sound out
the Pensacola Strutters Ball, twelve boxes
of La Petite matches in an oblong box marked
"Maine Cranberries Lick Colds." Tan, terrific,
Nita-Naldi-eyed, our Clara Bow foot-shimmies:

> I went to Coney on one of
> the cruise boats
> the summer I felt quite
> the Alice Adams
> in my organdy flimsy and no
> beau. Rik-i-tik-i-
> tik, doe-doe-di-doe, pranced
> the lizard loungers
> from off their two-tone feet
> on a beer-green sea-
> side boardwalk ballroom floor.

Coney. It is like a brother, the carious-toothed ocean mouth
salivating pee and babies. Coney. The morganatic husband of a brewery
heiress seated at her electric organ to guests' guffaws (how was she
to know?). Coney. A hundred million boys at Herald Square mark
Armistice Day on the unlined pages. Coney. Proud Yuletide cheer
loudly claims the scavenged nickel. Coney. We never go there anymore.

> Jane, won't you take your shoes
> off, or something? Are you turn-
> ing those pages with a hoe? Jane.
> In the name of the name of . . . Hey!

JACK FROST SUGARS

The East River, tidal,
strolls uptown, the color of a fish.
Shadows of cloud and smoke
vanish on blond brick.
Smoke stacks are clumped
in rows like spring asparagus spears
in cool October

that, barely,
has bronzed the shrubs and little trees
along the little lawn,
distance smooths out like a light-green sheet
darkly stripped by the UN Building.
Spume drifts
look like snapping from an egg whisk.

Letters that say JACK FROST SUGARS
at the Jack Frost dock in Queens
whitely return the gold
of a horizontal sun
this rainy morning, so grimy
and sodden. Hidden in overcast,
an onion tower or steeple
so far—it must be Brooklyn by then—
is now discriminable.
Downriver, by the delicately webbed gasometers
and the antennae, frailly tensile,
lumber kindles into golden flames
curling like shavings from a plane.

I didn't know they closed
            the Washington Market.
No more (it's years since)
            subway safaris
to New York's best butchers,
            admiring looks at
grizzly-bear steak (if it tastes
            like boar, you can keep it)
or half-and-half and clams.
            They swept up the sawdust
and closed it (it's always there
            one imagines to go back to)
forever. Quite an ugly building,
            not inside. It felt ancient
in Washington: is it twenty-five years
            since they tore it down,
sold the handmade bricks
            for replica houses?
Scrapple, hogshead cheese, Maryland
            peaches, Winchester apples,
the fingernail-on-blackboard squeak
            (O Chesapeake!) of oyster-
shucking, shopping by pecks and bushels.
            Shed markets
became an affectation to the too few:
            like milling your own meal.
I like oysters better now than then
            and ice cream
doesn't taste as good as the rhubarb
            kind a farm woman used to freeze
with her own hands, raw from cold,
            and rock salt. She'd be
about seventy if she's still alive.

WHERE WAS I?

on Greenwich Avenue
staring down Jane Street
into the sunset
out of which
walks Joe Brainard

HOT NIGHT, AVENUE A

Eluard died thinking of the Rosenbergs

le dur désir de durer

KIRK DOUGLAS   BARBARA RUSH

KIM NOVAK   ERNIE KOVACS

Strangers when we meet.

        I'm all right Jack

      roses in the slot
      a water carafe slops
      on carbon paper
      when is a man not in danger

the night is passing
passing and I, like
Sappho, lie alone
      "in such a night . . ."
who'd care to lie
by dank drawers and a sweaty T-shirt

      soaring in Roman crags above its locusts
      lours beneficent Stuyvesant Town

A WOMAN ON A ROOF

Surely I'm not going to tell you it's gray, or silvery
or think of the right word to color the weather
                    "the crepitating etc." V. Woolf

So if I send you a red-felt tomato, much-used,
with a strawberry stuffed with grit attached to it,
much stuck by rusted needles,
you'll know it's my heart

or I could ask you why River House has a hat on its cake
and four stone candles around the cake, of which I can see three

or if I tell you, "You must change your life!"
you might never read Rilke again.

Listening to the excitable music, it's funny
how the childhood moralities
in movie houses seemed to come true:
he murdered his wife and got away with it
for a few years while the pressure on his chest grew greater
and the spongy matter in his lungs consumed itself
until he had just breath enough left to say, "Hello," and die.

If the news only were really news!
"Say hello, I don't want him to think I'm avoiding him."

Hello, I don't want to tell you anymore about anything,
I want it to happen! You can call it Mexico,

this roof where the ventilators have on tango hats,
fungaceous and exuberant together.

It's so pretty, all this tar and bricks
and down there on their terrace two contented lesbians
taking turns lying in their gingham hammock

but I'm serious
about wanting to think of something really witty that will
            make you laugh.

Not today, it's too gray
and I'm too happy because I can say
"at least I am not *un*happy"
what a sappy way to feel.

Look at all the bushes in the sky
and not say what I want to say
it's too true and would sound like
                "your head on my shoulder,"
                "you twitched in your sleep,"
                "it's all you."

SHORT POEM

My muse plays tennis
and has a body like a Greek god.
My muse wears glasses
and looks swell in them.
I could go on like this forever.

SLIGHTLY HUNGOVER SUNDAY

when it's too soon to focus. Last night's party.
We played games.
Adverbs. I was a defrocked priest.
The fried chicken was scrumptious
and so were the greens and black-eyed peas.
A girl with a blond braid
did the twist very badly and told me
she understood my problem. And me,
happy as a clam! Wasn't I there
and not at two other parties? Parties
are nice, but a lot depends on
who's giving them. Now little headache
I'm going to sleep you away.

MAKE MOCK

At Minetta's I say, Bernie, you
played your guitar in bed. Strum
strum. I danced Saturday morning's
fandango. Your obese father came
crying threats (of course he didn't
say a word, he never did). Did Bob
misunderstand my misunderstanding
about mat fans? Now who puts freesias
by Hortense's photograph? (It seems
wicked, the second wife should have
the first wife's photograph.)
The candelabra flung itself on the carpet.
Let it untwist (I hate writhing) and say,
in many ways, it was a mistake to grow up.

HECTOR

There you were, selling tickets
at the museum, covered with blood and gold dust!
I exaggerate. A few glitterings,
metal and winier than wine clots, that cut eye.
Yes, you were everything:
nose and arrogance, a style of clothes
that seemed to say something
but didn't—the way I like it. O Achilles,
I already invented cracks
in your armored heel while we were at the giggles
and you-love-it-too? stage.

POEM (HELP ME)

Help me
find the paradox I look for:
the profoundest order is revealed
in what is most casual, these humped and cat-
ty-cornered cubes, the wind,
so you're planning to be sad
or casual
as a hat
off a yacht,
afloat
in a cove.
The wind puts its hook in.
The yacht swings at its mooring to face out to sea and into it
(the wind) a whippet with rabbits in mind.
Planning to go
pick mushrooms &/
or blueberries—or raspberries, or gooseberries.
What do you
think about
when you take
a walk? Goose-
berries at Pea Point—
peeing at Gooseberry Point; or, "I'll be cross as two sticks if
I don't outlive _____!"
Stones stick up through grass.
I am in love with July.
The canoe
takes a snooze. The rowboats
poor things
they have piles and
cannot sit still. "I must be mad,"
Emory Lovell said the other day,

"or very tired
when I think I like wild plum by night."
Write
Edith a sequel.
Writing
John,
Thanks for the
free copy of
Remembrant's *Three Trees*
but have some already. "the dog is chewing on
his bark (pun)."
In younger lesser days liked
skinny birch; now
I like scratchy juniper which won't pretend to like you
from whose berries
fragrant gin acquires
a savor—happy hours
bars in Amsterdam
when the cold days
cast iron lids
on Dutch ovens.
                    ". . . Not like clump birches—."
                    What's so great about a short-lived tree?
Oh. They're all right

to get you doughnuts

                    Dear Pat'n'Ron, when I leave the window open in
                    that room on a day like this (the wind is whipping
                    up some gray whipped cream) a blade of air goes
                    through the closet (the door to it is closed) into this
                    closet (back to back with closet #1) (also closed)
                    and strikes "like a dagger in your heart."
                    Tell Wayne not to grow up so fast. Some of us huff
                    and puff a lot running to keep up.

and when I think
of Frank and I do
a lot, my head
wants to burst
with unshed tears
                    Go ahead and cry
A natural place to stop
but nothing stops
nothing to show
a name on a stone
in a prestigious boneyard I don't admire
better stop
            the wind won't let me
most beguiling and perverse of men.

YOUNG O'HARA

—Those bricks there?
—These woodwinds here.
—You are a square, aren't you?
Frank cursed the driver's boxer (leave alone
my perp) and the sun broke the rain. But
this is Frank's story.
        An act of flesh obliges me,
        like dinner does, to defecate.
        I'm so depressed, and yet
        again a Chinese puppet soirée.
        "When you want what you see,
        see you then what you want?"
        The czar's guitar unstrummed petti-
        coats, laced beached women.
Frank danced, swam, moralized, joshed, frankincensed.
"There's always room at the top!" and "We're all in
it together." Where could an elevator go but up? He's
in the air, like our good G, distilling of nuns' tears,
the ball of the foot, of the bead of light, of the razor
slashing wire window screen. Friends' fresh crimes.

Up to her—waist—in roses and honeysuckle, Jane
in the shadow of the Pharos, quitting Alexandria
said, "August in the country, winter in town. What
I need is a new skirt for my vanity table. Pinned
with frat pins, the old one tore like an expurgated
page from an adultress's diary." Sexy, chaste, a noon
moon (Diana's cuticle, Molly Pitcher's pensive
penciled 'brow), suggested pedicures and penny
whistles; Jane felt a need of what was new, new. True,
in style, to the muses' blues, unsandaled footing hot
sands, up and up, the dumpy dunes bragged a dopey view
of elms and water. "I'm not content. I will get paint
on my dress. I thought I was beyond these thoughts:
I know my secret. I don't envy me myself, but I'm not
surprised if you do." Such statements revolt the natives.
Jane painted a radio so real it played.
Coiled in the seed in the earth,
the shoot that will separate the sunporch floor,

Jane looked so pretty Thursday night.
Gloriana of the treehouse tavern and
the films, she was seen giving Frank
a new meaning. No mean semanticist,
she binds the dough.

TO KENNETH KOCH

"Drinking a morning cup of coffee is one of the pleasures of peace,"
I thought as I drank my morning cup of coffee while reading
            The Pleasures of Peace.
"It is also one of the pleasures of war," hinted a still small voice.
"A *what* kind of voice?" Oh, all right, a small voice from a still.
(In truth, a white coffee biggin in which I infuse morning coffee
            essence.)
"You evade the issue," kindly stated S. A. Schonbrunn & Co. of
            Palisades, N.J., 07650.
"A morning cup of coffee is a pleasure of peace
which will also prove savorful in time of war."
"In other words what you are saying," clattered Miss (1 lb.) Yuban,
            peering yellowy into her cup,
"is that there are also pleasures of war."
"By no means," affirmed the Marzo Maggio Medal on the Gold Medal
            coffee can.
"Coffee—black Italian roast by preference—is all things: stimulant,
            anodyne, palliative.
It drives the husbandman to work and mends the homely housewife's
            busted TV set in time for *Edge of Night.*
It speeds the Avon representative with a kindly word.
It irons the cat's pajamas.
It collects old labels which it sends to friends and other shut-ins.
In one cup of it lie all the colors that ever were, blending in searing heat.
It gives the soldier strength to fight—"
"Ha!" and "Alack," I cried, and started from the wooden chair.
"Off, fancies, off! Vain imaginings, begone!
No more to the biggin will I hie
but take these frittered pence—see, there's this, & this, & this—e'en with
            them buy
a samovar, where of whose amber fluent flux, though it cheers not,
            nor yet inebriates

night's phantasms—maychance begot of the gorgonzola-faced and
fruitless moon—

in the dawn flaunt. Yet
stay. I'll once more to the licorice spring and sip, or, hap'ly—
should the god-lurched and enspruced nix so deem—gulp
a cup o' the morning, its blackness lightened to a passing tan
by a little something out of this gallon carton (Covered by One Or
More U.S.

Patents 3,116,002, 3,120,333, 3,120,335 Other
Patent Protection Pending)
of Wight's Dairy pasteurized homogenized vitamin D milk

400 U.S.P. UNITS VITAMIN D PER QUART
Bucksport, Maine ★ Tel. 469-3239
and lace it liberally and well with Sailor's Warning.

THE VILLAGE

I hate Greenwich Village like Vachel Lindsay said
                      somebody's always throwing bricks
what's Allen Ginsberg got against Vachel Lindsay?
Dear Allen:
              just to've thought of
              "The Eagle That Is Forgotten"
is quite something. And sincerely I admire you
and haven't a clue
when you say "poet is priest."
                    "binding with briars . . ."
haven't you read everything? Even corny for fun?
I suspect your favorite painter is Balthus.
"That's a terrible thing to say."
                  Now you will think I don't like Balthus.
Didn't you ever look at *Blue Poles*
and want to wade in the man-high fishy-eyed surf
or tell that Noailles poet-lady Vuillard painted in bed
             "move over"? Anna de,
who wrote about gladioli and borzoi:
that's what I mean: her poems can't be any good:
        they might be but think of the fun making them up,
imagining how they smell
        of the kind of perfume a woman who would rather talk
        than eat wears,
you go big for Americana: where
is Vachel Lindsay buried anyhow? He used to give readings
        in the Hotel Mayflower in Washington,
        which is like finding a fat book in a tank full of trout.
        Allen, it's Sunday, and like the song
I just dropped by to tell you,
        I hate the Village and like you,

and what you said to me once
at the San Remo, may it burn to the ground,
and—
honest injun—
poets are people.

NEVSKY PROSPECT

Those Russian poets, quarreling and
weeping into trains to go where sun-
set oozed hot as rosin and the gnats.
Force and evil? *Je ne comprends pas.*
Firs, beeches, uproar. A high-collar
blouse, a deck chair, lions and eyes.
Sweet tea, sweet champagne, poverty's
knotted snout, rank field flowers:
trees whipping midnight's suns: Nevsky
Prospect. Me and the little woman
suck poisoned words in the Ivy Book
Shop much like Trotsky and Lenin in
London on a gray British Museum day.

SEMI-ERUDITE

after Roger Shattuck, The Banquet Years

Quasi-inspired

very calmly ecstatic

near beer

      "Did you ever sleep in the Colosseum in the rain?"
Gregory Corso's cigarette burnt low. He left
The American Academy in Rome
for Venice.

          A possible mistake.

I hope he is at least as ingenious as Casanova.

A fabulous New York ennui
floods me like the it-looks-like-snow-but-its-not-cold-enough day
semi-erudite

          O

the worst word in English
the first in primers and novels for children with 17-word vocabularies

          O

I suppose it means *yoni*
I can speak plainer than that
in the short words kids use because they're hungry or happy or
      "my hanth cold, my feetth cold, an' I hathta pith"
or, to a plein air painter painting the smog-loaded light
      "It's O.K. to eliminate if you want to, mister?"

O

get Gregory Corso out of Venice

POEM (PATRICIAN AS A BALD EAGLE)

Patrician as a bald eagle
or lamb leg with mint sauce,
the night-owl trolley shimmies
outer suburbs bound from heart
of Scranton. Or is it Scranton?
Melodious mistake, it's Florence!
They are talking Italian. You
are thinking English. Val d'Arno
wind, cold as a witch's knee,
full of rain. On the glass.   ·

THE GATE TO THE LAKE

Rain quilts the river where it resembles
a Swiss lake. The further shore is spotted
by millionaires; while they live, one knows
so little of them. And a bridge will span
three miles further; they call the pergola
Amalfi. Rain laces the cutenic waterfall
with other laces, the rain-warm pool looks
mountain-cold. How tame, how trivial, how
grand the water, a delicate twig, it
fell, when?

A WINDOW IN THE QUAI VOLTAIRE

Water curls under the bridges
and among the tree trunks
whose bottoms, above the earth, are under it:
it's not a river, it's a flood.

The sky has a few ridges.
A few people sample books.
More walk beside the flood and look at it:
is it bad or good?

Cloud ridges cut the sun in wedges.
It sets. Some drunks
fall in the river and drown in it.
No one who saw it will forget the flood.

AMSTERDAM

Although on fine days she still likes to wear
the bracelets of her yellow elm leaf
floating, divided into links by bridges,
hemicycular canals (much as one might expect
the women of these crow-step gabled pinched
brick houses to wear, on fine occasions,
jewelry "in the family" since
the seventeenth century),
it is the middle of October: winter begun
and Amsterdam belongs to the clerk in black,
who, with briefcase and a bunch of crimson roses,
boards the sadly lighted tram,
withdrawing from the far-off dying sunset
station square, as night
clangs down and into place (proving
that cold is not a wind, but an iron lid).

SEASONS

Climbed with unholy purpose
holy stairs, by a cypress
the simple blasphemy. Grape-
green moonlight on a wine-
red damask bedspread. The
nightingale song: movement
and stasis, that a way of
life is a way of death. A
string shopping bag, cab-
bages, sausages, savour
of day-to-day swelling
Jacopo's bronze doors at
Bologna: creation and fall.

Unmorticed loosely fitted
stones, straw and candles,
on the Rome road. A cute
church! Refinement of deso-
lation, pink and sulphur
teatime fog on stone, on
a Bailey bridge splintering
beneath jeeps, bikes, carts,
feet. A beggar knelt at an
approach, blew on a grass
blade, "Lili Marlene." The
nightingale whistled another
story: name, fact, act.

BERNINI

Not one of the first, the inventors, the wonder workers,
Yet, water-born, he took what was theirs and there
And from it worked his own:
Let fountaining water fall among figures
Gesturing freely as the water sketched
At the height of its jet,
Changed jets to obelisks,
Bubbled the fish-scale domes,
Made doorways and windows bloom like lotuses
On the water-flat faces of palaces,
Cast, like a net's cork floats, a colonnade around St. Peter's fountain.

From the blown conch-shell water foams
In the tangled, stony water world of Bernini's Rome.

SONG: FROM OUT HERE

Eat your hay, it's gray grape-treading time.
Too many mornings bring the telephone:
all the way from Rome to
tell about goats on a cisalpine hill!

Buses, buses.

Two daft young things parking a
lush zoo spell in a go-go cart.
She: Why don't they let the yak out?
She: The sun stuck its tongue out, Kate.

Na'theless, the city has its use,
the country its cloud drops, sad
belch-belly cows, a hill or three.
I think we understand each other.
Honey, with money we'd trip, but
O enchant me a sentence like, O
smile!

FRAGMENT (PLEASURES AMBIGUOUS AS DINNER)

Pleasures ambiguous as dinner in Zurich after too
much lunch in Rome, or ennui-ed to death by a dead sea.
The sour lemon's seeds cracked sweetly bitter, light
spread its hair on the tranquil lavender, houses scattered
among the terraced orange trees, above the church
and fishing boats with wide eyes painted at their prows.

FOREIGN PARTS

Meat-eater, salt-licker, piped spring
dribble-sucker, an exiled Bolshevik's

villa at Viareggio. The beach sheep
shit crumby money, munificent marks,

lire, dollars, Dolorous Daintyfoot,
Proudass, Chinadoll, a three-way clut-

ter, the piazza pizzeria. Mrs. Smith-
Jones, rich, gonged aground a pissoir.

At three the imprisoned poisoner's tea
tells her rice-cake fortune, it is it.

Who to who? You yew alley ewes knew
goatsuckers in Swedish horsehide hid

the boathouse key, locked the oarlock,
sung Sam's nutsy song, "Sin Fleet," at

night. Night, ketchup cup, pepper-pot,
bid bound Belinda break her bracelets:

the dirty photographs apostrophize mon-
soons. Swimming snakes shake the lake.

A LETTER

Among the Inca stones of
grandmother's mountain hovel,
at the helm while peach petals
out of the sun make bird tracks
on the backs of combers, dawn,
I mean, all the time,
I think of you deep in me.
You are very sweet and cute.
You are luscious and blue-eyed,
what my Indian ancestors
saw in my Spanish forebears.

STELE

The ocean twisted gods' cocks like
washcloths. Some centuries pass.
Dorcas wades the mountain, knee-high
in oak and poison oak. Apollo pissed
a rainbow and Dorcas, smoke, climbs
his thigh, coiled in the frightening
triangle tangle. The world looks odd.

St. Theresa strokes her breast.
The nipple exudes tears.

Night. Come-strung as a slack string
harp a hand wipes a mouth of husks of
kisses and smears the sheet.
Bloody shit.
A woman hangs out heavy wash.
Mechanics are on their backs.

I will suck you off in Athens
and carry your seed in my mouth
to your friend at Syracuse.

TO ONE SLEEPING

Creep into my arms wounded modern one
and have my seeming safety and real warmth,
we nesting birds, we pungent foxes,
and I will kiss away
the night and morning and an afternoon
that withered like wildflowers that won't be picked.

Visit me by telephone, "Hel-
lo," a broken greeting and snow
your shy affectations in my eyes
and I will magnify the snowflake beauty of your shyness.

Come to me at my place of business
call on me in squalor, my kind's
pride, O honorable sloth, careerist,
my love, my only hope to hold
you is that in me which you can't understand,
which, in a secret way, in you, only I know how to find and touch.

I laughed at your sicknesses.
I will kiss your vanity.
I forced your ugliness on sweet ones
of a deeper ugliness, like foulness
in the finger-ends of gloves, the tips of scabbards.
I will praise you, your speech and vulgar air,
your jaunty air will from a heat of praise,
my praise, burst like wild gladioli into veined purple bloom.

CATALOG

bloodroot and shy hepatica
                    tall violets
                    in thin grass
                    at the edge of a wood

trout lily
or dogtooth violet

                    speckled

gullies

                    what other flowers are there?

wild flags, rank daisies, black-eyed susans in Laurentian meadows
                    suns

                    dandelions, buttercups

                                        unsheltered
                                        wild roses

beaches, roads,
chewed, pink, pollinate
                    whitest blackberry
wind-tossed elderberry

                              tiger lily
                              blazing tiger lily
                              sings so loud

PULLING CRABGRASS

The joint stems rooting
knotted and matted in the soil so the stems snap,
leaving the irritating canker
to sprout anew, while odd larvae
tumble into light, curly striped gray-brown ones
and shiny lacquer red,
kind of repulsive, an earthworm's crawl
has a familiar friendly wriggle.
Then, a flattened-out place,
a cat has made its summer siesta spot,
a dusty gray-and-white puss,
lanky, underfed and hip
to city ways, nibbling that grass tip,
with a sooty, backyard quality.
One at a time,
the cleaned roots and leaves of grass, gather
into a Watsonia Peaches bushel,
then, when it's ready for the trip
out to the ash can and to be trod down,
it looks like a harvest
festival of succulent green sheaves.

IN SHAD ROE TIME

One word is too often profaned
for me to feel stuck-up about using it
if I mean it even if I used it
when I didn't or changed my mind
          "listen, sweets"
the tulips—

          "Once I turned my back on some
          for a moment and they completely opened."—

are of two sorts

modest, faintly penurious,
pale, lipped with red except that one
has a green stripe
               and
voluptuously deep and burning
can two reds be so unlike? purple's afire
in the craters of these giant parrots

who'd've thought they come from
one and the same shop
the spring it rained six continuous days
in foggy Yorkville

YORKVILLE

These, surely, are the unwholesomest whores of all!
"Don't let *her* see us
getting into the car. *She'll* tell Helen."
Your doctor can tell you.
You are largely a matter of food.
Sign on a sausage palace:
"On this site stood
The Gloria Palast:
longtime home of
gemütlich sex comedies
with lederhosened lager lappers
who laughed and bumped
against each other. It smelt
of marzipan."
Papa's danse-thé ist nicht tod.
Hail, thin-walled high-rise apartment house!
Here shall we live
(It *is* the parents' fault when children have bad teeth),
here shall we lead a life like that of the common dodder
—"Sorry I backed into you, sport"—
"black sheep of a proud family"
"cousin of the bindweeds."
The last of the electricity
—though for all our intents and purposes electricity
is immortal—is consumed, having
"given up living
in an orthodox fashion, from the soil,
leafless, scale-bearing, drinking the life sap
('What are you supposed to be?
Go take a haircut.')
of its unwilling host,

if which perishes,
it also must die."
Dead Elevators
Juicelessness: A Study
The Elevator Mania: The Middle "Modern Times" Phase
"Elevator, hand control, mint condit., complt. wh. orig. rubber matting.
Will accept best offer."
Flowing along, broad and buxom
Yorkville, trying to learn
not to hate nobody, trying not trying,
eating a hamburger with a loaf of bread wrapped around it,
drinking a glass of fresh Love Squeeze
each city has its own beauties and vilenesses
—loneliness, standoffishness, views—
unable "to utilize fully
the wonder of the young"
known in some places as "the love vine"
elsewhere as "angel hair"'
some "fall to the ground,
sink into the soil,
or float off into the water to found new colonies."
Bang! You're gone.
And in each city,
each quarter—each neighborhood, that is—
is individually flavored
however uniform. Any man or woman in uniform
can tell you this. Yorkville,
that tastes like an asphalt thorn apple.

AN UNDATED POEM

Written in a room with California wildflower paper:
to the tune of Jerry
practicing to a metronome;
to the sandy sprinkle of rain
on a trumpet vine; to cars
that accelerate and pass;
to the silence of Anne cooking,
the not-so-silence of Kate
teaching Liz
to swing and play the *sacrifice*
(there is such an instrument:
a red, white and blue recorder
that looks like a saxophone);
Fairfield's hammer, in certain rat-a-tats,
Suzanne's name called
"*Su-zanne!*" "*Su-zanne!*"
and chiming clocks.
      Jenny clipped, sheep-shape,
full of old wisdom, flops
and snores.
      A triad on the *sacrifice*:
Supper portends—
      and I haven't written
you what I wished to write—
      there's time.
      A room where you've slept,
Obscure Destinies by the bed,
flowers on the wall
of the state where you are,
dear friend
               le plus charmant des amis de Fabergé

kissy traveller,
here on Lawrence's gold-oak desk a golden deposit slip
        on May 13 '60
you made a cash deposit
        $75.00
I send you what I can never take away,
        you needn't accept.
There is no one quite like you.
                Would you care to wrestle
                or shake hands?
Here in the East
        it's supper time
                I—
                        no, I won't write it.

one word is too often profaned
                you might understand how I mean it
                        dear mutual friend

INFORMAL NOTE FOR A GREAT BIG FORMAL ODE
ON MY ONLY SUBJECT, YOU

Quite as unexpectedly as though a pigeon had flown in my face
on a street in Cambridge a few weeks ago I thought I saw you:
just as instantly as I thought the stranger coming toward me was you,
I could already not at all see the resemblance my unprepared eyes
had seen.

Cambridge, almost level with its lovely Charles, will always be sunny
for me with the flashing of your quickest passing.

I get to feeling so excited and silly,
I want to say things like, you're too good to me!
greedily.
You are so good to me
that even my own feelings don't make me feel guilty.
You don't know how rare that is for me.
You do know
probably though,
who are so perceptive and sensible.

IT'S NICE INSIDE WHEN IT SNOWS

Self-conscious and up-to-date,
kissing by lamplight,
whatever it was, it was not for that,
whatever it is, it is not for this.

These are ugly chairs.
These are comfortable chairs.
This has an unnecessary dimension.

Its name is necessity.
Its name is beauty.

Firelight eats shadows in the wall.
A mirror in the hall
shows firelight shining from wall to wall.
Firelight devours the mirror in the hall.

They hold each other.
They laugh, kiss and tell
what they have themselves
to tell, or not to tell.

UNDER A STORM-WASHED SKY

The grass is a yellowing green,
ready for the bleaching snow.
The shadows are violet blue under the hedges
of forsythia frenziedly whipping their canes
in the wind and the trickling sunlight
that lured out one, no, two blooms that grip
and ride the intimate tempest like bees
blazing with pollen. The big gray house with the white trim
shows on its shadowed side as violet blue, too.
An elm and its shadow are one.
The twigs of a pear tree are knotted
and glazed with light. The clothes pole
stands empty of purpose, a faint green
on its shadowed side. A cloud like a slice of mist
slides under the sun and the shadows momentarily fade
in a thinner shadow that spreads over the grass.
The trumpet vine has been chopped back
to bursts of stumps of stalks.
The wind eddies and veers, drops and lifts
just the branches of a sycamore
and shakes its seed-ball ornaments. A dog
and a puppy lope on the lawn.
If you spoke in your sleep and said,
"We are dying!," at any rate,
we are not dead. Life goes on.

in her Playtex girdle that holds her shape
after six months of continuous wearing
Modess because somebody
lovely just passed by her
hair in 7 Party Colors

                            raspberry puce ocher blue mutation
ermine by day and fox by night

space-shoon with a rubbery gait
a stylish stout more bounce to the ounce
she passes out
                a jug

of Joy

        zum

reach me my Windex
with a powdery nose
whatever became of Joyce
Wedgies and my old pal
Enna
Jettick?
           not to speak
           of Bernice Tunafish

                        world's costliest perfume.

JO STROLLING THINKING

See Jo slap the shopping bag sway
of her Etruscan hips, hold out
the egg, the only egg, the liveliest.
Crack its thought and eat it up, Jo
knows. "My summer in Toronto I got a
taste of paper cones of chips, French
fries, served with a wooden skewer.
Refined as bar sugar or Lido sand,
a fine moral sense of a religious
sense of life exposed a dirty photo:
my sixth pearl tear might well be
fake. I am listed in a list. I care."

Sunrise, rose of a sun, the sun
rose and Jo kissed the derelicts'
leper lips and tucked into the park
the derelicts under a cinder sun.

"My purse is full of bees. Plant,
moon leg, a star foot in my armpit
honey hive. 'The little gray leaves,'
Lanier said. Then I ghosted *Tiger
Lilies*. At cock-crow sank the bottled
olive boat. There are no more olives
on the little hill." Jo's magic herbal
hooked a fish wish for we who are
alone together. Fine blighted flesh,
Jo stabbed coconut eyes, flowed
atoll milk on the coral stranded.

"Who can save who cannot save?" "Life
must change us who are it and cannot
change. I would open the cinder rose,
the sun, like a napkin wrapping rolls."

DREAMS, ANNIVERSARIES

Four years ago today Jo left 12th Street:
five years from tomorrow on what tripping step
her heelless scuffs (mules)?

> "The mixmaster juices
> mother's rotten oranges,
> whips tears. Are these
> leeches or black bread
> crusts. Each named wave
> flips ashore some lucky
> one: me, one day, he
> said, 'I won't, again,
> nylon sand socks hurt.'"

Jo scribbled her dairy diary accounting
butter and egg men small loss. Toted colonial
nights, taxis, taxes, lilies begetting rain.
"Fagin initiates Oliver to crime-life: me."
At home, in bed, alone, scrawled, Fagin day.
But the ailanthus shakes tent-caterpillar feed,
showers rinse glasses, most men are helpless
foundered in sex like the Krakow crystal into
water. Trumpeter, what trumpet you? Winged Jo
thinks the jewelly night, mother's a letter.

> "Ho hum
> bums
> at my
> sigh
> die."

DUFF'S

The sky in here is very blue
and made of wood.
You are very great,
I think.
Ruth is great.
Have a brandy.
Nobody lives forever
and it's a fucking shame.

JIM MORRISON

of The Doors
fame the Ad-
miral's son hit
the enfevered deck
burning: pee-
no'm-nee-a
its wiggy name.
Goodbye Jim.
I remember him
yelling
singing, sig-
naling
waving a hand-
ful of meat.
How proudly
we hail! Dying
and living
salute you
dead. Wave on
Jim's dong.

THE WATER GARDEN

Angelica Kauffmann unlimbered her easel on a step.
The King of Naples's sword flapped his thigh. Bent,
seemingly like a pencil.

The American's yacht floated. Whiter than white,
the white evening capitulated an orange oxbow.
So. She paints, she spits.

Simian ogresses discuss tarts' parts. Pearl-stuffed,
his majesty's magisterial cucumber vends salad days
to vegetarian nymphs' swains.

A bird's bill closed on Angelica's brush like a rat-
trap snapping shut on a rat's neck. "I will finish
my portrait another day."

The king stands in a pool the color of a cocktail.
He is sad, he is royal, he hunts. He built the Taj
Mahal and sold it.

The very city there is here, the very green plums.
Music shakes the gold dates on the gold date palms
of the royal box. It was.

WINTER DATE

"Turning the floured fryer in the spider
in the hot snap fat, your mother's hands
like the golf course under snow
under the moon," said Antinous to Lulu,
"Park your carcass by the caddy-house door.
Lulu, your breath vapors, as the wind lifts
powdered snow sanding the moon-dune crust
blue tonight and green. Our cheeks, cold
stung as hands, fat snaps at
turning fryers, surround like sherbert
the roasts and suckling pigs of kisses."
"The crust, the crust, Antinous! When I
was a child," Lulu said,
"we made angels flat back on the snow."

SONNET

The look of the light makes me think of travel.
In my woolly head thoughts ravel
and snarl, faintly, like cries
of one who, sleeping, dreams and sighs.
The day is colorful and pale
and dying. Boats on the river sail
down toward the harbor to flirt with the sea
and the thought of travel, like me,
who sits and pretends to write,
waiting for the fun that will come with night.
The night will come and bring regret
for what I've planned and not done yet.
The hell with it. The fainting light
as it dies in waves grows bright.

DESTITUTE PERU

for John Ashbery

We pullmaned to Peoria. Was
Gladys glad, Skippy missed
Sookie so. So Peru-ward, home.
"I'll sew buttons on dresses yet."

Nike's peach-knife nicked little
finger Chinese straw finger-cuffed
to Minna's Siamesed. Hartford,
how are your wheres, our whens?

Or extirpated traumas' gifted
guilt smothered aboard a club
car. Lake Ontario spilled
Jo Jo's knapsack: "Pasternak."

An alligator ate an alligator-
trapping monkey. We ate because
"it's dark, it's air-conditioned"
like lurching to the movies,

shot marbles in lobbies. What
interests? Takes? Escapes? Eat,
moth-light, part and apart, slowly
we slow waiters serve hot plates.

THE DISCOVERY OF AMERICA

Succulent garbage-knots
an eyeline 'twixt galley
and gull—grapefruit,
sots. *Lisboa* stared us
to sea, who cast off old
threats (a tooth like a
bead, sweet smiler) held
a wave in its track.
            Kris Kringle set
a crab free ashore, took
to wife a syphilitic boy's
bright princess. Feathers
in the carts of Spain,
lisp as you pass saints'
betters, querulous, tough,
the bandit ransomed: more
yes than *no*, propping
a rock in rock valley.

Really, these sea trips,
all sailors and all whose
ships while and when you,
you know, for must, return.
A scholarly queen financed
the sand with a hocked bell.
Her consort, Jaime, hails
to her dead hands *nouvelles*:
"Own and only, on you feast
the extinction of temples."

CHANTEY

Now how who won all know
the game's for the tell-
tale teller. The spice isles
gemmed the ocean groin
nicely, hove to view, slack
sailed. "This dressing's
to be changed: bite
the tube." Pain unfurled
like paper. School of schools
Sargassan, eel us home.

Vixens blunder the bluffs
pink palms shelving moustache
eyebrows: girls, girls, girls
us await. Yes, *oui*, us.

Necessity invented intention,
that without which then
coupling's a loose-lip joiner.
Philosopher's tone, dancer's
prance, sway down the briney.
Tropics. Trance. Pines.
Morgan. Smith. Jones.
The ice-stream phosphor of
sea beasts, coffin the fathoms.
We abroad no more.
Time shrinks in shell.

THE SMALLEST

It is in front of the tree.
The houses around the windows are lit
by it, it turns off and goes upon
knees and wherever the bone is almost next
to the skin. It has been defamed.
It will become undernourished.
It is not without end. It is not.
It is not what you can let happen,
or cause to happen, or has anything
at all to do with happening.
It happens as it exists without effect.
It is the pure in pure mathematics.
It is the sully in unsullied rain.
It is the pain in painfully.
It is also the fully. It is
the light in highlight and headlight,
the head in headland, the towering
in towers, trees, the outstretched
in shadows of mountains on plains and lakes.
It is not the water in the lake, however,
it is not cupped.
If it exists, it is unaware of it.
It could name itself however, and does.
It contains alphabets.
It is infinite and therefore the smallest thing.

THE WEEPING BEECH

hangs down into the day,
so hot, so bright, the very bridal
of an August afternoon,
a Sunday afternoon,
the limp and leafy branches,
which are not like a branch,
stirred slowly, only there
and then they stop. This is
a hospital: weak nerves
have brought me here among
majestic trees bringing to
therapeutic sessions
an intensity like when I
write. The heat wave may
never end. Sweat-soaked:
a rash: salt on skin: intolerable
itching. Beside me
a zinnia, a pink gold-hearted mum,
one white carnation, a sprig
of pachysandra flowering
minutely.

TWO VOICES

Crystal flowers explode
blue rain, I read, violets
reign the rain flame.

Scriabin's sonata ends.
Whitman said, *merci, en
masse*, amiable partner.

Take your lips with you,
hips and haws crackle
cracked stepped stone.

Livid lips, say yon photo
lies: through what unview
saw you my jaguar?

You're a brick, weak one.

Flesh, flash.

Miss me?

Locksmith.

Dream punched sortilege, gut
peeler, hideously apropos,
rosy apothegm, roll.

Acropolised home, sainted
larkspur quails a dung bug's
afflictive creep.

Cut mist
sink to sob.

Hemlock wound with bay.

Forestalled.

I stay. I go. Still
silver spoons
scoop wax apple shrines.

WHERE IS INDIANA BROWN?

Two of Father Feeney's Slaves
        black, silver crosses
appear, lift the bride's veil,
show us her kisses.
The one with the poodle
tastes of honey;
the other one,
        a honey-colored poodle.

They lay on a bed, all three,
three men lay on his bed crossways,
a tree climbed up,
what a warty, gray, gay tree!
My, what a nasty, cold, wet night!
Ole Bull picked up his violin,
fiddled *Pages from an Indian Diary*
he had gone so far out of his way.

Golden earth, an aspect of
a forgotten journey.
Our spoons came from Woolworth's,
sexual deviations.
Chance acquaintances, the crying sisters.
The listening house.

THE NIGHT

passes and I can't sleep, I who
have been dropping off at ten-
thirty, and waking up at seven.
Insomnia, "always my torture."
I sit and smoke and stare and
drink can after can of Fresca.
I think my thoughts and remem-
ber wonderful sex with my ex.
Talked to the guy upstairs
yesterday, he's pretty attractive.
Asked me what I did and when
I said poetry and novels he
said he'd like to read some
some time. And so you shall,
my dear. I wonder, I wonder.

TO AWAKEN

with a stuffed head and
blow my nose on whatever's
handiest: perhaps the wing
of this passing morning
angel, flying in the room.
And look and see between
my toes protruding from
the ugly cover (huge orange
butterflies and giant daisies)
a tousled head and a nose:
pointy but not too pointed:
why, it's Tom! He must
have spent the night, and now
gets up and goes to pee,
the first of many pees he'll
take throughout the day.

"And if I carry (she reflected)
the mark of a beast on my left
breast, what of that?" Repairing
a lock at midnight, her wolverine
lover's roommate woke her and
old St Pat's bells tolled the hour
they were not meant to, its graves
foamingly light. She shuddered,
and drew the covers, sipped
port. He came. He said, "Go into
bed, I will think of you there
till the mending's done. What a
mess this couch is." "Drain me
in a kiss! If hell is my dream
of a tunneled throat and skipbeat
cartoon men I'm scared, love."
While the dawn sung masses
their hearts waxed and waned
separately dreaming dreams they
met in. She made the bed. All
day, doors creak on hinges.

POEM (THE DAY GETS SLOWLY STARTED)

The day gets slowly started.
A rap at the bedroom door,
bitter coffee, hot cereal, juice
the color of sun which
isn't out this morning. A
cool shower, a shave, soothing
Noxzema for razor burn. A bed
is made. The paper doesn't come
until twelve or one. A gray shine
out the windows. "No one
leaves the building until
those scissors are returned."
It's that kind of a place.
Nonetheless, I've seen worse.
The worried gray is melting
into sunlight. I wish I'd
brought my book of enlightening
literary essays. I wish it
were lunch time. I wish I had
an appetite. The day agrees
with me better than it did, or,
better, I agree with it. I'll
slide down a sunslip yet, this
crass September morning.

FIVE O'CLOCK

Men disport themselves.
They help each other:
"Reach in my chest and massage my heart.
I am not dead."

If clouds are God's table linen,
what is rain?
He gave men towels to dry themselves.
He blessed their soap.

The city grew like the desert, by erosion.
Men walk in it.
God is not so much dead as resting.
His seventh day has just begun.

Men step out of the wind.
They give money and necessaries.
They steal what belongs to them.
The eighth day, doors open on new sights.

Men in hats rise from the ground:
Bless these broken dolls and mend them.
What goes through cloth, walks and floats?
We rise lightly in you.

THE EXCHANGE

The mind dies down.
Nerves, unsheathed, stir.
Radios. A water tap.
Depart, flesh, trailed
by barbwire hair. Sea salt
explores lips of lacerations
cut on you like a christening
nick. A yellow light
in blue light. Twilight
and hydrangeas watery
through hedges. Was the hideous
lesson worth the pleasure?
Unmouth your secret.
A fishy curse flaps
in the gunwales. Kissed
gooily, a goodbye-kissed head
and a door, coffin shaped,
to the closet of the fields,
field of flowers, sea
and city. More perishable than glass,
eyes break looks and pocket
them like coins, tribute
for the trip back.
Flesh of flesh, senses
spoke judgments minds
left unformulated. Smell of flesh
secretions scenting flesh.
Sheets drifted to the laundry.
The laundry at the bottom of the street
which is the sea.
Air shattered upon its curbs
and signs and aimless destinations.

POEM (FISHES SWAM IN THE FIRE)

Fishes swam in the fire, as
a miraculous pussycat
dipped paw and caught a
cold coal and the flames
chuckled, the fish swam.
Green towers of a seaweed
city drowned in lava
flowing sunset, dawn,
liquid, crisp, gilding
the gliding cripples
crutches into soft solid
gold: a jackknife cuts
like lead, sold, melted
down, buys newness in
heat. The fishes swam,
the pussycat crouched,
the city switched its
flamey lights, clouds,
banners, its crowds surged
in a pond's weeds ebb-
ing to the powdered ashes
morning slow snow flow.
Gray! fall, faint white.
The seaweed city skeleton,
a fossil fish in coal.
The pussycat sits in the
window, paws under, watches,
wonders, waits, cat
tracks in the field, fire-white
sun in the crystals.

POEM (WHETHER SCHLEPPING BOOKS TO AFTER-CLASS DETENTION)

Whether schlepping books to after-class detention,
or weeding,
or turning a handle to a trainer's "bay"
in August, Key West,
while the jock itch itched,
or at sea, foam, slap, foam, slap,
or a couple of stories up
above Sixth Avenue's racket in the Jersey April drift,
or at the shore shoving sleep aside,
(why is it wrong wearing wool britches in light weather?
the wool the sun spins)
for "who sleeps by day," rid
of the creative afflictions, fled,
leaving an empty-fortune cork,
that tastes of rice water and glue.
It's almost impossible
to think about absolutely nothing
without getting a headache.
On the other hand,
a reasonable facsimile thereof . . .
yes, that could be arranged.

Terror of three-in-the-afternoon
when the head sinks
toward the typewriter keys
and five-thirty looms
in the sandy distance of the beach-flat afternoon
like a closed refreshment stand,
you are an old pal of mine.

I SLEPT, AND IN A DREAM

V. Sackville-West came to me and said,
"I can imagine a border
in shades of purple, pink and mauve
or, if that is too somber . . ."
I wake, and the moon
white beyond the somber spruces
counting the wrinkles of its waning cheek.

SMALL TALK

—I hear there's a drought.
—I can live without that.
—Did you see *Blow-Up*?
—I found it quite old hat.
—What do you think
  of the new morality?
—I think undergrads
  should concentrate on their grades.
—You may be right.
—I could be wrong.
—What a sweet
  thing to say.
—Compliments are never out of date
  if they're sincere.
—About the new morality
  I don't know much
  but I love
  the old sincerity:
  Are you for real?
—I guess I'm kind of
  out of date
  but right from the start
  I like to speak
  from the heart.
  At any rate
  let me feel your nose:
  A cold nose
  means a warm heart.
  My, your nose is hot.
—What's worse
  I've got cold feet.

—Cold feet?
    In those shoes?
    What kind of foot powder
    do you use?
—Dr. Scholl's.
—Well, that's the best.
    Have you tried
    lamb's-wool liners?
—I'm allergic
    to wool.
—So that's your Achilles' heel.

THINGS TO DO WHEN YOU GET A BAD REVIEW

Straighten up desk
            too introspective
go for a walk
            ditto
wash hair
            somebody else's
baked Alaska
            ugh
make transatlantic call
            mmm
tighten nuts, loosen screws
enlarge
deliquesce
write letters
            Dear Meager Sack of Shit,
forget it
but remember to
leave windpipe
"hanging over pot"
            and "let out any impurities"

THERE IS A CERTAIN SOMETHING

to be said for an economy of waste.
Unfortunately I haven't time to go into it thoroughly, but,
well, like the huge bowl
of shaving soap yesterday
I almost bought: "a shaving bowl"
that will last five years. It was turned out of streaky wood
and would strike its own note in my bathroom.
To think, on the eve of my fiftieth birthday,
I might still be swabbing a brush in the same
Floris's Rose Geranium—to go on and on, bitterly missing
scent after scent, vetiver, lavender, mint, Barbasol.
Or to die, and leave a legacy
of shaving soap. It might make it more endurable
if I started shaving twice a day
though I scarcely need to, and two and a half years
is a long, long time: what about bergamot, patchouli, *l'heure exquise*
and Barth's Unmedicated? Not to speak
of Bouncing Bet, *Saponaria officinalis*, the common soapwort.
Or I could use the Grandfather bowl every other morning,
that might work. Great grackles, then it might last ten years.
Or just scrape it out when it got boring.
No, an economy of waste and conspicuous consumption are not
           the same,
I feel it in my bones in this hot apartment on the coldest day
of that ambivalent month, March.
And to think I used to be content to shave
with mere cake soap: Palmolive, Ivory, Packer's Tar.
Perhaps I will stop shaving
and let my nose grow.

FOR REASONS NOT KNOWN TO ME

Poems are written under many conditions. —John Ashbery

The sun has come out
and I am taking a bath.
No, a shower.
There is a giant jar of instant Sanka
on my desk and
a bottle of Caron's Tabac Blond
(from Paris,
by way of J.A.).
For reasons not known to me
I have five drawers of shirts
and . . . oh forget it.
For reasons not known to me
Bella Abzug came in fourth
in the mayoral runoff
and Koch and Cuomo are
running neck and neck
(I do not give a pickled fart
about politics, elections,
professional liars and
all the rest. I hope Koch wins.)
For reasons not known to me
I have persuaded my mother
to have an operation
which will remove the cataract
from one of her eyes:
she is eighty-seven and
reading is her main resource.
Sometimes Christian Science
strikes me as slightly silly:
I have never met one who
did not go to a dentist or

wear glasses if they needed
them, come rain or come shine.
And that's that. Goodbye.

WE SEE US AS WE TRULY BEHAVE

We see us as we truly behave. —John Ashbery

1
We are wrapped in our shawl
and wear our moon.
At our approach, the firs shiver,
seeming to know us.
It is not us. It is wind
their needles pass through.

2
Men passed by on horseback.
What is more beautiful?

3
When we were most sincere
and least. When we thought
what we thoughtlessly spoke.
When we said, "if I say,"
and forgot. Recalling
kinds of insincerity,
we see its truth.

4
He went off fast
on the thing he was on.
She kept shelling peas.

5
We cleared and cleaned
a high narrow room
and painted it white.

We freed its window.
Through the cracked pane
passed a cold blade
of air. At night
it showed a starry sky.

LIKE (SONNET FRAGMENT)

Like one pumpkin from among the corn shucks
risen into a cold sky's deepest blue;
or rolled in winter down heaped sea-chewed rocks,
like an orange, of those the changing winds strew;
ridging a river with its own white road,
the moon, full in a color of the rose,
on breathless night vibrant with croaking toads,
fainting, flushed, in oily tatters goes,
its face, stupid with distress and pain,
peering into cat-rattled ash-can yards;
or shy in dawn-green misty after-rain
like a puff at sea when a ship bombards . . .

SUFFERING

Its seed is in the college boy whose clothes
tell how the dumb imagine it as rags;
its poisoned breath is on the voice that nags
a child whose mother thinks that its life goes
toward where she found it no relief to weep;
and friends who stop their ears and scale their eyes,
like married ones who wrangle all their lives,
all dream its branches clatter in their sleep:
The fear of suffering burns like the sun,
and everyone turns from it, everyone.

Which is not true.

UNWELCOME SONG

After all, said and done.
No one, nothing won.
Gone from home, home.
The shiftless, shipped out.
The lonely laugh.
A crowd collects, a panner's nuggetless sand.
A crowd collects, nuggets a panner panned,
gold flesh that bleeds like bloodroots bleeding
pale-orange rust-red sap,
a spring wood,
a city of trees.

A handful of sand
in the wind,
in the eyes
and the eyes' globes bleed
gold-speckled blood
like gold-speckled glass
in a glass city, under the glass leaves,
a glass city,
a city of trees.

IN THE AFTER-DINNER LULL

for Barbara Guest

I listen to the news:
there is no news.
Goodnight, Walter Cronkite.

The sun sets only
as it does one evening
in the fall. Goodnight, sun.

The moon, will it be full?
I last saw it so
in September: goodnight, moon.

Look, I can't go on
standing on one foot
waiting for a moon
to rise. Goodnight, moon.

And goodnight to you
faithless reader, and
to you and you and you.

THE SETTING OF THE MOON

after Leopardi

As, in lone night,
above silvered fields and water,
when a breeze plays,
and distant shadows make
a thousand vague aspects
and deceptive objects
among calm waves
and branches and hedges and small hills and houses,
arrived at the confine of the sky,
behind the Apennines or the Alps or into the infinite
breast of the Tyrrhenian Sea,
the moon sets; and the world grows colorless;
shadows vanish, and the dark
hides mountain and valley;
blind rests the night,
and singing, with a sad melody,
a wagon driver salutes the last ray
of the fled light
which before had led him on his way:

so is taken, so
from mortal years, goes
youth. In flight
are the shadows and shapes
of delighting illusions; and less often come
the far-off hopes
that prop a mortal nature.
Life is left
wretched, darkened. Casting his gaze before him,
in vain the confused traveler searches
the long road which he must take

for goal or reason; and finds
that the place of humankind
from him, as he from it, is truly estranged.

Too happy and gay
our miserable lot
seemed there above, if youth,
in which each good is of a thousand pains, the fruit
should last the whole of life.
Too kind decree,
which sentences each animal to death,
unless, first, half the way were bound
over to labor,
yet harder than terrible death itself.
Worthy of immortal minds . . .

TO HIMSELF

after Leopardi

Now rest forever,
my tired heart. The last illusion dead,
that I believed eternal. Dead. Well sent
to us of dear illusions
that not just hope, desire is spent.
Rest forever. Enough
palpitations. Nothing is worth
your effort, nor does earth
merit sighs. Bitter and boring
is life, never other; and the world is filth.
Quiet yourself now. Give up,
the last time. Fate, to our kind,
gives only death. Now despise
yourself, nature, the brutal
power that, in secret, commands all,
and the infinite vanity of all.

NOTES

3 **Invocation.** Undated, c. mid-1950s.

5 **Via della Vite.** Via della Vite is the noted thoroughfare in Rome.

7 **Mother's Land.** Beggar's *lice*, not *lace*, is the plant that Schuyler clearly is referring to here. The erroneous use is maintained, however, in keeping with the allusion to the "grandmothers' weed(s)" that follows it.

9 **Coming Night.** Dated December 1952.

10 **Light Night.** Dated March 1952.

12 **Blank Regard.** Dated 1952. Author's note: "This was about a book of pix of Marie Antoinette—*famille* in prison—you recall the late-eighteenth-century vogue of wearing a red ribbon *à la guillotine?*"

13 **East Aurora.** Dated 1952. The family moved to East Aurora, New York, a small town outside Buffalo, in 1937.

17 **July Sixth.** Dated July 1953.

18 **The Times: A Collage.** Dated May 1953. Using "collaged" text from *The New York Times Magazine*. On May 18, 1953, the aviatrix Jacqueline Cochran became the first woman to pilot a supersonic aircraft. She broke the sound barrier, flying 625.5 mph as she streaked across the sky over the California desert.

21 **Address.** Undated.
   Antinous—(c. 111–130 AD), lover of the Roman emperor Hadrian.

22 **Sweet Romanian Tongue.** Dated August 1952.

24 **Distraction: An Ode.** Undated.
   "Quale in notte solinga"—the opening of Giacomo Leopardi's last canto, "The Setting of the Moon," translated by Schuyler (p. 196).
   Recanati—birthplace of Leopardi.
   "the sea, far off there . . ."—from Leopardi's "A Silvia" ("To Silvia"), line 25: *"e quinci il mar da lungi."*

25 **Caniglia sang Norma**—Maria Caniglia (1905–79), one of the leading dramatic sopranos of the 1930s and '40s. *Norma* is the opera by Vincenzo Bellini.

26 **"broom"**—a yellow-flowered shrub and a crucially important image for Leopardi (see his great late poem "La Ginestra" [1836], also known as "Il fiore del deserto" [The Flower of the Desert]).

27 **Beautiful Outlook.** Dated November 1953.

31 **Gifts.** Dated 1953.
   Lena Hartl—daughter of the painter Leon Hartl (1889–1973). Written at Sneden's Landing, on the Hudson River (see note on "Le Weekend," p. 201).

32 **St. Valentine.** Dated 1952.

33 **Grousset's China (or Slogans).** Undated. René Grousset (1885–1952) was a French historian specializing in Asian history.

36 **Tears, Oily Tears . . .** Dated summer 1952.

37 **Scarlatti.** Dated April 14, 1957.

39 **Dandelions.** Dated March 26, 1957.

40 **So That's Why.** Previously published in *May 24th, or So* (New York: Tibor de Nagy Editions, 1966) in a different version (titled "Hoboken," with seven extra lines at the beginning of the poem and omitting the last three lines of this version). The poem was not printed in any of Schuyler's subsequent collections. The additional lines in the *May 24th, or So* version read: "I was going to write you a poem / about Hoboken and you playing Chopin / but I can't write it now. / you see all these frustrating things happen / I know exactly how I felt / how the poem felt when I was going to write it / you know, that was when I should've." Alvin Novak (b. 1928), pianist.

43 **El Médico.** Dated 1957.

45 **To Jorge in Sickness.** Undated. "[W]e are writing something together" refers most probably to *A Nest of Ninnies*, a collaborative (with John Ashbery) novel, begun in 1952, with writing continuing on and off up until 1969, the year of its publication.

46 **Jorge Pronounced George.** Undated. Presumably the same Jorge of "To Jorge in Sickness."

47 **Having My Say-so.** Dated April 28, 1956. Written about and given to the painter John Button (1929–82).

52 **I Am Keenly Disappointed. I Eagerly Await.** Dated 1957–58.

53 **Visiting the Kress Collection.** From the mid-1920s to the end of the 1950s, Samuel Henry Kress (1863–1955) and the Samuel H. Kress Foundation (established 1929) built one of the most remarkable private collections of European old master paintings, sculpture, and decorative arts ever assembled. Kress donated some 1,800 works to the National Gallery in Washington, D.C.

54 **What the Dealer Said.** Written c. 1957.

55 **Ace Bullcatcher: A Collage.** Dated July 14, 1958.

57 **Dim Diversions That Occasion an Exercise in Pure Thought Logical, Conclusive, Undemonstrable.** Undated. A significant portion of this poem (starting with the line, "The veiled lady has a story to tell," through to the poem's end, and with minor variants) was incorporated, as a prose segment, into the longer poem "Eyes at the Window" and was published in *Hymn to Life*. See *Collected Poems* (New York: Farrar, Straus and Giroux, 1995), p. 157.

58 **A Heavy Boredom.** Dated July 24, 1958.

59 **Turandot.** *Turandot* is an opera in three acts by Giacomo Puccini (1858–1924). *Turandot & Other Poems* was also the title of the first book of poems by Schuyler's friend the poet John Ashbery.

60 **Fanfare on a Dog-Violin.** Dated December 31, 1953.
    to telephone the folks / at Sodus—John Ashbery grew up in Sodus, New York. He traveled to Paris on a Fulbright Fellowship in the early 1950s and stayed until 1965. (See also "'Dedicated to G. Verdi. Because It's His Birthday.'," p. 61).

61 **"Dedicated to G. Verdi. Because It's His Birthday."** Undated letter-poem to John Ashbery in Paris (see also "Fanfare on a Dog Violin," p. 60).

Parties—novel by Carl Van Vechten (1880–1964), published in 1930.

La Modification—a 1957 novel by Michel Butor. The novel was translated into English as *Second Thoughts*.

Pixérécourt—René Charles Guilbert Pixérécourt (1773–1844), a French theater director and playwright.

F. T. Prince (1919–2003), English poet.

Lina Pagliughi (1907–80) and **Amelita Galli-Curci** (1882–1963), operatic sopranos.

63 **Letter Poem to Kenneth Koch.** Kenneth Koch (1925–2002), poet. Undated, but internal evidence dates it to the time John Ashbery was away in Paris (see notes to p. 60, above).

Hello Janice. Hello Katherine.—Janice and Katherine are Koch's wife and daughter.

the Moustache—Ashbery.

"fragrant May"—from Leopardi's poem "To Silvia" ("Day / after day you spend like that / All the fragrant month of May"). See also p. 199 note on "Distraction: An Ode" (p. 24).

64 **Le Weekend.** This poem was written c. 1952–53.

Sneden's Landing—an area in Rockland County, New York, home to Schuyler's friends the duo-pianists Arthur Gold (1917–90) and Robert (Bobby) Fizdale (1920–95). The dramatis personae here are Gold (Schuyler's lover at the time), Fizdale (Gold's duo-piano and domestic partner), Arthur Weinstein (a decorator and Fizdale's lover), John Ashbery, and the poet, "Jimmy" Schuyler.

66 **Kennexth.** Undated.

Kennexth—mocking a lisp perhaps, or a passing allusion to the American poet Kenneth Rexroth (1905–82)?

68 **Variations.** Undated. See previous poem: the presence of "gorilla" suggests the similar iconoclastic spirit of Kenneth Koch here.

71 **Birdland (or Caligula-Caligulee, or Come into the Garden Maud, the Grass Needs Mowing).** Undated, but internal evidence dates it to the mid-1960s. "Come into the Garden Maud" is an allusion to a popular poem by the English poet laureate Alfred, Lord Tennyson (1809–92).

Goodman Brothers—clarinetist Benny (1909–86) and his brother, bassist Harry. Schuyler has mixed up the Leopardi quote from "A se stesso" (1835): *"La vita, altro mai nulla; e fango è il mondo."* The full Valéry quote from *Charmes* (1922) is: *"Le vent se lève . . . Il faut tenter de vivre!"* The Latin is Propertius, Elegy 1.2, line 8: *"nudus Amor formae . . ."* The full quote from Racine's *Bérénice*, act 1, scene 5, is: *"De cette nuit, Phénice, as-tu vu la splendeur? / Tes yeux ne sont-il pas tout pleins de sa grandeur?"* The final quote is from *Merchant of Venice*, act 5, scene 1: "In such a night / Stood Dido with a willow in her hand / Upon the wild sea-banks, and waft her love / To come again to Carthage."

Noia, Princess of Bavaria, / crushed beneath the windshield of her own Thunderbird—the character (a contraction of "para-noia," perhaps?) is seen here to be an amalgam of "the Mad King Ludwig" (Ludwig II, 1845–86) and the 1950s pinup and movie star Jayne Mansfield (1933–67).

72 **Sentence (*or* Sentences).** Undated.

Cat Cay, and Towser—Cat Cay is an island in the Bahamas, once notorious for pirates. Towser was a common name for a dog. Perhaps Schuyler wanted to end this poem by punning on the phrase "cats and dogs"?

73 **Just Away (*or* Jonquils Approach).** Dated August 4, 1955. An acrostic on the name of his friend John Ashbery. (See also "J Is for My Name," p. 74, and "Far Off," p. 75, both also experimenting with this form.)

74 **J Is for My Name.** Dated September 2, 1960. Another acrostic, this time on the name of the critic John Gruen and the painter Jane Wilson's two-year-old daughter, Julia.

75 **Far Off.** Undated. An acrostic for his friend Frank O'Hara.

76 **A Blue Shadow Painting.** Dated April 8, 1961. Dedicated to Schuyler's close friend the painter and art critic Fairfield Porter (1907–75).

77 **Water Lilies.** Undated. *Water Lilies* (or *Nymphéas*) is a series of approximately 250 oil paintings by French Impressionist Claude Monet (1840–1926).

Penobscot Bay—in Maine. The location of this and of several subsequent poems is the Porter property on Great Spruce Head Island (see, for example, p. 100, "Great Spruce Head Key West").

85 **Evening.** Undated, but was one of a batch of poems Schuyler submitted to *Accent* in 1951. (See also the poem "Amsterdam," p. 139.)

86 **Untitled.** Dated November 10, 1967.

88 **Soft Sawder Skies.** Dated November 27, 1967.

90 **Thanksgiving.** Dated November 1960, Southampton.

Lizzie and **Kates**—Elizabeth and Katherine Porter, the two daughters of Anne and Fairfield Porter.

93 **New Year.** Undated, but internal evidence dates it to the late 1950s.

Hortense Schneider—popular French soprano (1833–20).

Gertie—Gertrude Lawrence (1898–12), popular actress and musical comedy performer. While on tour in London in the 1920s, she introduced the hit "Limehouse Blues."

94 **Poem (We all lay on the island beach together).** Undated.

Brian—Brian Howard (1905–58), a poet and critic and (most famously) one of the madcap Bright Young Things of the 1920s in England. Despite great promise and flamboyant charm he never produced the masterpiece he and others expected he would.

the redhead—Howard's lover, Sam Langford (1925–58).

Bill—Bill Aalto (1915–58), Schuyler's lover for a time, with whom he moved to Florence (see editors' notes).

Wystan and Chester—poet Wystan Hugh Auden (1907–73) and his partner, Chester Kallman (1921–75), who knew Schuyler and Aalto in Florence.

95 **Impromptu: Dorabella's Dreams.** Undated. "Dorabella" was Schuyler's chosen "camp" name.

96 **Seemingly by Chance.** Undated, but internal evidence dates it to the mid-1950s.

Quai Voltaire—see p. 138.

posters / we laughed at: **Frères Lissac**—a popular poster for these famous Parisian opticians by the artist Capiello portrayed a man being fitted for spectacles, though it might mischievously be misconstrued as an image of a sailor receiving fellatio!

Albi—a town in southern France, famous for its Toulouse-Lautrec Museum.

97 **Chabrier.** Undated. Alexis-Emmanuel Chabrier (1841–94) was a French composer.

Gerhardi's lips—William Gerhardi, later Gerhardie (1895–77), British novelist and playwright.

Firbank—Ronald Firbank (1886–1926), English novelist.

98 **Leonards Lake.** Dated April 8, 1970.

99 **From the Island.** Dated August 1964.

100 **Great Spruce Head Key West.** Undated.

effebo—slang term (from "ephebe") for young, effeminate gay male.

104 **Welcome.** Dated March 7, 1966.

106 **April.** Dated April 30–May 1, 1978.

110 **Poem (As I came by the swimming pool).** Undated, but internal evidence dates it to the early 1950s.

111 **Poem (The sun stands still a sec).** Dated August 20, 1969. Schuyler contemplated calling this poem "Closed Gentian Distances," then shifted that title to another poem that he published in *The Crystal Lithium* (see *Collected Poems*, p. 102).

112 **To J.A. in Prison.** Undated. To John Ashbery. The prison is metaphorical, of course (his exile in France?).

113 **Jane Sculpts.** Undated. To (and about) Jane Freilicher.

Nita Naldi (1867–61) and **Clara Bow** (1905–65)—two of the most successful screen actresses of the silent film era of the 1920s.

Alice Adams—eponymous heroine of a 1935 film starring Katharine Hepburn.

Coney—Coney Island, the seaside playground for working-class New Yorkers.

116 **Where Was I?** Dated July 17, 1969.

Joe Brainard (1942–94)—American artist and writer. His prodigious and expansive body of work included assemblages, collages, drawings, and paintings. He is perhaps best remembered for his innovative prose memoir, *I Remember*, and his iconic "Nancy" drawings. A version of this poem appears in *The Diary of James Schuyler* (edited by Nathan Kernan; Boston: Black Sparrow Press, 1996, p. 70), undated, but placed c. September 8–15, 1969. "[A]m I / where was I? / up above Greenwich Avenue / looking down into Jane Street / into the sunset / out of which walks / Joe Brainard."

117 **Hot Night, Avenue A.** Undated, but internal evidence dates it to 1960 (the poem's capitalizations represent the marquee names of the principal actors in the film *Strangers When We Meet*, released in 1960).

le dur désir de durer—a 1946 volume of poetry by Paul Éluard (1895–1952). Éluard, one of the founders of the Surrealist movement, joined the French Communist Party in 1942 and became an avid Communist.

I'm all right Jack—a reference to the Peter Sellers film *I'm All Right Jack* (1959).

"in such a night"—Schuyler quotes one of the great Greek lyric poet Sappho's fragments ("I lie alone") here.

Stuyvesant Town—a housing complex in New York adjacent to Avenue A.

118 **A Woman on a Roof.** Undated.

Rilke—German poet. "You must change your life" is (in English translation) the famous last line of Rainer Maria Rilke's (1875–1926) poem "Archaic Torso of Apollo."

121 **Slightly Hungover Sunday.** Dated January 7, 1962.

122 **Make Mock.** Undated.

Minetta's—Minetta's Tavern, a famous Greenwich Village bar.

124 **Poem (Help me).** Undated, but internal evidence (the death of Schuyler's friend Frank O'Hara) dates it to 1966.

125 **Pat'n'Ron**—the poet Ron Padgett (b. 1942) and his wife, Pat (and their two-year-old son, Wayne).

127 **Young O'Hara.** Undated. See also lines, quoted in the editors' notes, from "Poem (Help me)" (p. 124) and Schuyler's acrostic poem on O'Hara, "Far Off" (p. 75).

128 **Alas for New Haven!** Undated. For Jane Freilicher.

129 **To Kenneth Koch.** Dated August 19, 1965.

The Pleasures of Peace—Koch's 1969 collection, *The Pleasures of Peace and Other Poems*. See also "Letter Poem to Kenneth Koch" (p. 63) and "Kennexth" (p. 66) in this volume.

131 **The Village.** Dated December 20, 1959. The Village is New York's legendary bohemian Greenwich Village.

Vachel Lindsay—American poet and troubador (1879–1931). Schuyler here alludes, in his opening lines, to two of Lindsay's poems, "Factory Windows Are Always Broken" ("Factory windows are always broken. / Somebody's always throwing bricks) and "The Eagle That Is Forgotten" ("Sleep softly . . . eagle forgotten . . . under the stone / Time has its way with you there, and the clay has its own.").

Allen Ginsberg—American Beat poet (1926–97).

"poet is priest"—from Ginsberg's poem "Death to van Gogh's Ear," which had just appeared, the month previously, in *The Times Literary Supplement*.

"binding with briars . . ."—from a poem by Ginsberg's hero, William Blake (1757–1827), "The Garden of Love": "And binding with briars my joys and desires."

Balthus—Balthazar Klossowski de Rola (1908–2001), a French painter.

Blue Poles—Jackson Pollock's (1912–56) legendary abstract canvas.

Edouard Vuillard (1868–1940)—French Postimpressionist/Nabi painter.

that Noailles poet-lady Vuillard painted in bed—Anna de Noailles (1876–1933), a leading literary figure in France in the pre–World War I period.

132 **the San Remo**—located (in 1959) at the corner of Bleecker and MacDougal Streets, in the heart of Greenwich Village, one of only two literary bars that mattered in New York City. The other was the White Horse Tavern.

133 **Nevsky Prospect.** Undated. Nevsky Prospect, the main thoroughfare in St. Petersburg, is Russia's most famous street.

134 **Semi-Erudite.** Undated, but internal evidence dates it to the late 1950s.

Roger Shattuck—*The Banquet Years*—the classic study, published in 1968, of the Parisian avant-garde from 1885 to World War I, known as the Belle Époque.

yoni—the Sanskrit word for "source or origin of life"; it can also mean "vulva."

135 **Gregory Corso** (1930–2001)—youngest member of the inner circle of poets associated with the Beat Generation.

138 **A Window in the Quai Voltaire.** Dated January 19, 1955. See also "Seemingly by Chance," p. 96.

139 **Amsterdam.** Dated c. 1951 and one of a batch of poems Schuyler submitted to the magazine *Accent* (see also the note on "Evening" [p. 202]).

140 **Seasons.** Undated.

Jacopo's bronze doors—Jacopo della Quercia (1374–1438), a major sculptural innovator of the early Renaissance. Schuyler is referring here to his reliefs surrounding the portal of the Basilica of San Petronio in Bologna, which he visited in 1948. In calling them bronze, he may, however, be confusing them with the Lorenzo Ghiberti panels for the doors of the Baptistry in Florence (to which della Quercia also submitted a panel, now lost)—the San Petronio reliefs are marble.

"Lili Marlene"—a famous World War II song made popular by Marlene Dietrich (1901–92).

141 **Bernini.** Undated. Giovanni Lorenzo Bernini (1598–1680) was a preeminent Baroque sculptor and architect of seventeenth-century Rome.

150 **In Shad Roe Time.** Undated.

Shad Roe—the Cole Porter (1891–1964) song "Let's Do It, Let's Fall in Love" includes the memorable lines "Electric eels I might add do it / Though it shocks 'em, I know / Why ask if shad do it? / Waiter, bring me shad roe."

One word is too often profaned—the title of a poem by Percy Bysshe Shelley (1792–1822): "One word is too often profaned / For me to profane it." That word, of course, is "love."

151 **Yorkville.** Dated June 30–July 7, 1967. Author's note: "with some phrases from *National Geographic*, July 1922." Originally appeared in *Angel Hair* 5, spring 1968. Yorkville is an area on the Upper East Side of Manhattan located around Eighty-sixth Street, famed in this period for its Central European restaurants and bakeries.

The Gloria Palast—one of Yorkville's most popular restaurants in its heyday, which had not only a German movie theater on the main floor but also ballrooms for waltzing and polka dancing.

153 **An Undated Poem.** Author's note: "written on a Saturday in August, 1960." This poem was composed at the home of the Porter family (Jerry, Anne, Kate, Liz, Fairfield, and Jenny the dog).

Obscure Destinies—a 1932 omnibus of three stories by Willa Cather (1873–1947).

le plus charmant des amis de Fabergé—"the most charming of Fabergé's friends," refers to the Imperial Russian jeweler Peter Carl Fabergé (1846–1920), creator of the Fabergé egg. See also Schuyler's poem "Fabergé" in *Freely Espousing* (1969).

157 **Under a Storm-Washed Sky.** Dated December 8, 1962.

159 **Jo Strolling Thinking.** Undated.

'The little gray leaves,'/ Lanier said.—Sidney Lanier (1842–81), American poet and novelist. "But the olives they were not blind to Him, / The little gray leaves were kind to him" is from "The Golden Wedding of Sterling and Sarah Lanier, September 27, 1868." *Tiger Lilies*—Lanier's novel of 1867.

162 **Duff's.** Dated January 1975.

163 **Jim Morrison.** Dated July 1971. Morrison died on July 3, 1971, in Paris.

164 **The Water Garden.** Undated.

Angelica Kauffmann (1741–1807)—a Swiss Neoclassical painter. In Rome in 1783 Kauffmann painted the large-format commissioned portrait *Ferdinand IV, King of Naples, and his Family*, an ambitious work depicting the king, Queen Marie Carolina, and their six children as life-size figures against the backdrop of a bucolic park landscape.

171 **The Weeping Beech.** Dated August 3–4, 1975.

172 **Two Voices.** Undated.

Scriabin—Alexander Nikolayevich Scriabin (1872–1915), a Russian composer and pianist.

Whitman said, *merci, en masse*—Walt Whitman (1819–92) in the poem "One's Self I Sing" from *Leaves of Grass* writes, "One's-self I sing—a simple, separate person; / Yet utter the word Democratic, the word *En-Masse*."

174 **Where Is Indiana Brown?** Undated.

Father Feeney's Slaves—Father Leonard Feeney (1897–1978), an American Jesuit priest who, in 1953, was excommunicated from the Catholic church for refusing to submit to ecclesiastical authority. He continued preaching and founded a band of followers known as the Slaves of the Immaculate Heart of Mary. See "The Slaves of Leonard Feeney" in *Time* magazine, January 1, 1965.

Ole Bull—Bornemann Bull (1810–80), a virtuoso Norwegian violinist and composer.

175 **The Night.** Dated April 17, 1975.

176 **To Awaken.** Dated October 10, 1982.

178 **Poem (The day gets slowly started).** Dated September 8, 1975. Written and set at Payne Whitney Psychiatric Hospital, Westchester (see also "The Payne Whitney Poems" on pages 252–58 of the *Collected Poems*).

183 **I Slept, and in a Dream.** Undated.

V. Sackville-West—Vita Sackville-West (1892–1962), English aristocrat, author, and creator of the famous gardens at Sissinghurst in England.

184 **Small Talk.** Undated, but internal evidence dates it to the mid-1960s.

Blow-Up—the award-winning 1966 British-Italian art film directed by Michelangelo Antonioni, starring David Hemmings.

186 **Things to Do When You Get a Bad Review.** Dated December 4, 1969.

187 **There Is a Certain Something.** Dated March 17, 1967.

l'heure exquise—in addition to being the name of a perfume, *l'Heure exquise* also alludes to a line by the French poet Paul Verlaine (1844–96) that became the title of a famous song by the composer Reynaldo Hahn (1874–1947) containing one of the most well-known French melodies.

188 **For Reasons Not Known to Me.** Dated September 9, 1977.

the mayoral runoff—Ed Koch (b. 1924) defeated Mario Cuomo (b. 1930) and the flamboyant Bella Abzug (1920–98) that year to become New York City's new mayor.

195 **In the After-Dinner Lull.** Author's note: "written in Tower Nine at Roosevelt Hospital, NYC, October 7, 1977." Barbara Guest (1920–2006) was an American poet and critic, and a close friend of Schuyler's.

196 **The Setting of the Moon.** Undated. Giacomo Leopardi (1798–1837) is among Italy's most revered poets. "Il tramonto della Luna," his last canto, was composed in Naples in 1837, shortly before his death. Schuyler's inspired translation here breaks off about two-thirds of the way through the poem.

198 **To Himself.** Undated. Translation of Leopardi's "A se stesso," written c. 1831 in Rome.

ACKNOWLEDGMENTS

We would like to extend our most sincere gratitude to the people who've supported and aided us in the process of collecting and editing this book: Lynda Claassen and Robert Melton at UCSD's Mandeville Special Collections Library and Archive for New Poetry, Jonathan Galassi, Nathan Kernan, William Corbett, Trevor Winkfield, Peter Gizzi, Eileen Myles, and our various friends and families. A grand thank you to the executors of the Schuyler Estate: Tom Carey, Raymond Foye, and the late Darragh Park.

INDEX OF TITLES AND FIRST LINES